SUMMER OF SARA

ALEXANDRA RUSCH

Copyright © 2023 by Alexandra Rusch

All rights reserved.

No part of this book may be reproduced in any form or by any electronic or mechanical means, including information storage and retrieval systems, without written permission from the author, except for the use of brief quotations in a book review.

ISBN: 979-8-218-17905-2

For Jeff and my Scrapdawgs

CHAPTER 1

I smelled the ocean before I saw it, or even heard it. The top was down on my '67 VW Beetle, the wind whipping the strands of hair that had escaped my ponytail. As I turned off Route 35 and approached the beach, the sound of the waves breaking reached my ears. I pulled the Bug into the driveway leading to the place that was to be my home for the next four months.

After stopping the car, I pulled the hand brake and turned off the motor then sat and stared at the gorgeous home in front of me. Rising three stories above me, the Pendleton stood in all her glorious splendor, bathed in the light of the warm afternoon sun.

I resisted the urge to pinch myself. This incredible beachfront home was going to be mine for four whole months... the entire summer: June through September. I rented the Pendleton sight unseen, apart from a few photos available online from the realtor. The only condition I had was that the home must be beachfront. And beachfront I got. Gorgeous was a happy accident.

A few more moments passed while I sat in the Bug, wrapping my mind around everything happening to me. My life had done a complete one-eighty when I turned fifty-five, and change was not something I was known for handling well. In the span of one year, my marriage ended, the dentist I worked for retired, I moved into a small condo rental, and was, at this moment, trying to decide who I was going to be when I grew up.

I, Sara Maloney, age fifty-six… starting over.

Grabbing the door handle, I stepped out onto the paver stone driveway. I dug down into my huge hobo bag for the house key I'd dropped in there after signing the rental papers. The key opened the back door and I walked into the hallway that led to a stunning bathroom, large bedroom, and state-of-the-art kitchen. The living room came next and then I spotted the enclosed front porch with three walls of windows.

The early June sun streamed in, and I tugged the windows open to let in the ocean breeze. As if I were dreaming, I continued my tour, still not believing this was happening. How incredible was this summer going to be? No worries, no time constraints, no responsibilities… all the time in the world to soak up the sun, read, write, craft, and heal.

Upstairs, the second floor offered a living room, bathroom, and two more bedrooms. The third floor was a huge open space with a few twin beds, a queen bed and a perfect view of the bay. The house was gorgeous, decorated with the best of everything. The owners had spared no expense when it came to furniture, carpeting, moldings, granite countertops, and tile floors.

The main floor bath was huge, almost as big as my entire condo back home. The shower was a walk-in, no walls or doors or curtain.

"Okay," I said aloud. "First things first." I needed to get my suitcases, boxes of art supplies, laptop, and the groceries I'd picked up out of the car and into the proper spot. But the call of the ocean was too great, and I unlocked the front porch door, kicked off my flip-flops, and headed outside. I walked down the boardwalk to the main walking boards, which formed a T at the end of my walkway. When I reached the end, I turned around and looked back at the Pendleton.

Again, I was mesmerized by the beauty of the home and noticed how pretty the homes surrounding it were. Sloping dunes, seagrass, and pots of fresh flowers were everywhere. By summer's end, I knew they would be overflowing the pots with rainbows of color. Reds, pinks, blues and purples, yellows and oranges, my artist's brain went into hyperdrive. Making a mental note to remember to water them every day, I turned back to the ocean. I had to walk about thirty feet to get to the actual beach entrance.

The beachgoers wouldn't start for another week or so, after school let out. The sun was hot, easily 80 degrees, a gorgeous early June day. The sun glinted off the ocean and a few fishing boats were visible.

Strolling back to the house, I noticed only a couple of people walking the boards. An older couple passed me, smiling and saying good afternoon. I smiled in return and was surprised that it was a genuine one—I was actually happy. It had been a long time since my last genuine smile, and it felt good.

After walking around the side of the house to my car, I grabbed my suitcases, boxes, and grocery bags and lugged them inside. I returned to the driveway and pulled the car into the garage. Back inside the house, I put away the food and drinks, opening all the cabinets and inspecting every inch of the kitchen.

I laughed ruefully at the meager fixings—the refrigerator held my coconut milk, water, and a fresh bag of ground coffee. Some prebagged salad and salad dressing and a dozen yogurts completed the picture. The freezer held my frozen dinners and favorite blueberry ice pops.

Glancing at my suitcases, it dawned on me that I needed to choose which bedroom would be mine. I laughed because I could sleep in a different bed each night for a week. But ultimately, I chose the front bedroom on the second floor. The windows looked out at the ocean and the breeze coming in smelled of salt, sun, and sand.

I collapsed backward on the bed, once again resisting the urge to pinch myself.

A car door slammed nearby, followed by an excited bark. Flying off the bed, I almost fell down the stairs in my haste to greet the originator of that bark. Molly, my four-year-old golden retriever, was standing on the back steps, smiling at me through the glass door. Golden Retrievers have the best smile, Molly's mouth open, tongue hanging out and her lips curled up. I'd rescued her three and a half years earlier. Apparently, some harried young mother had given in to the pleas of her children and purchased Molly from a breeder, quickly finding out that a three-month-old golden needed more attention, guidance, and training than she or her young family could offer.

I ended up the winner in that situation, scooping Molly up the moment I laid eyes on her. A few months of obedience training and I had a best friend. I opened the door and she rewarded me with happy whining, tail thumping, and more than a few kisses. Molly acted like it had been twenty-four months since I'd seen her, instead of barely twenty-four hours. Unfortunately, I had to deal with the person who brought her to me.

"Thank you for bringing Molly," I said coolly, looking into the eyes of my ex-husband Ron. "It was very nice of you to offer to do that." I had been struggling with the logistics of suitcases, supplies, and Molly all fitting into my Beetle. Ron solved that problem by offering to keep Molly overnight so I could pack and close up the condo, and then he would drop Molly off with me on his way to an Atlantic City excursion.

"You're welcome, Sara. You have quite the place here…" He trailed off. "Why did you rent something so… big?"

As usual, with one question Ron managed to make me feel like a misguided twelve-year-old. *Ass* was the word that sprang to mind. "I specified beachfront and my price limit and this fit both criteria."

I knew Ron was focused on the cost of the beachfront

rental, but he had no right to question it. Although it was none of his business, I'd made it quite clear to him that the home was paid for with a very generous gift Dr. Reeves gave me upon his retirement. The doctor's only stipulation was that I had to spend it, not bank it, and treat myself to a vacation or trip: something splurge-worthy. So, I was merely following orders. The amount was generous enough that I had plenty of spending money for the four months and wouldn't have to dip into savings while I was staying at the beach.

As Ron was about to say something, the sound of a car horn interrupted him. Actually, it was quite comical. Ron opened his mouth and a car horn came out. It was truly apropos since most of what he often said sounded like a car horn to me. Rolling his eyes, he waved in the direction of his BMW, signaling that he was coming. I glanced over at his car, a gorgeous dark blue sedan, and chuckled when I pictured him trying to gather up all of Molly's long golden hair off those plush dark seat covers. I'll bet he regrets that offer, I thought wickedly.

In the passenger seat I saw the beeper of the horn. Bronwyn Caruthers, all five foot eight of blond loveliness was perfectly framed in the windshield. I'd never been perfectly framed in anything, and this broad could do it just by sitting in a car. Bronwyn waved her manicured fingers at me. I waved mine back. Of course, my manicure consisted of smoothly filed nails with a coat of clear nail polish. My fingers got too inky and adhesive- and paint-stained to warrant getting a real manicure.

Ron managed to look uncomfortable, like he thought I'd be angry and jealous that he brought his girlfriend along. Little did he realize, I couldn't have cared less. He cleared his throat and again opened his mouth to speak.

Molly chose that moment to bark. I collapsed in giggles, wondering what sound would come out the next time Ron attempted to speak. "Thanks again, Ron. Enjoy AC and tell Bronwyn I said hello." I started to turn to go back into the house. Ron reached over, and I mistook his attempt to pet Molly as an attempt to touch me and drew back quickly. Too quickly. The backs of my knees hit Molly and I fell backward, striking my elbow against the stairs.

Waving off Ron's outstretched hand, I stood up and brushed sand from my butt and tears from my eyes. "I'm fine, I'm fine," I mumbled and quickly ducked into the house. I watched from the kitchen window until my ex-husband and his girlfriend pulled out of the driveway. A big whoosh of air escaped my lungs. I hadn't even realized I'd been holding my breath.

I knelt on the floor and hugged Molly. I'm not sure there could have been a better cure for what ailed me at that moment than a Molly hug. Humiliation over my public clumsiness, embarrassment over my fall in front of Bronwyn, frustration with my ex's condescending attitude, all wiped clean with one huge wet dog kiss on my cheek.

I'm not sure how long I sat there, my arms around my best girl, my head resting on her solid body. Molly had an uncanny way of sensing my needs and she sat quietly while I held her and let my fears of what was to become of me flow out. "Thanks, girl," I said, ruffling the featherlike fur on her ears. "How about a treat?" Molly's tail thumped the floor in answer.

I tossed her a bone-shaped dog biscuit and she caught it midair.

A quick glance at the clock told me it was after 5:00 p.m. No wonder my stomach was growling. I hadn't eaten since breakfast, when all I had was a cup of coffee and a bowl of cereal. Choosing a frozen dinner, I entered the time on the microwave and glanced out the kitchen window. The house next door was close—maybe twenty feet separated my kitchen window from what appeared to be their kitchen window. I wondered if it was a rental and if I'd have good neighbors for the next few months. I said a silent prayer that there wouldn't be a ton of small children. The thought of screaming toddlers and toys and mayhem was enough to send a shiver of dread through me.

With that thought in my head, I noticed movement in the window opposite me. After a glimpse of someone walking through the room, I couldn't tell whether it was a man or a woman. *Well, at least you have someone nearby,* I told myself. Molly and I ate our dinners, and after I cleaned up my few utensils I snapped on her leash.

"C'mon, girl. Let's explore!"

With Molly's leash in one hand, a plastic baggie in the other (just in case!) and my cell phone and keys in my pocket, we set out for an evening stroll. The sun was descending on the bay side of the slender strip of land we call the Jersey shore. Growing up in North Jersey, my summers were spent in various rented bungalows in Point Pleasant, Lavallette, and

Seaside. I knew this area like the back of my hand and loved every square mile of it.

As we walked past the house next door, I noticed something that had slipped by me on my previous walk, scaffolding all along the street side of the two-story home. *Uh-oh. Maybe that's why my rental was so affordable.* Looking around the property I noticed some extension cords, ladders, and spackle buckets. As if the scaffolding wasn't enough proof, the other items cemented the fact that some type of construction was happening right next door to me.

I was an early riser, so morning noise wouldn't bother me too much, and late evening would be past working hours, so my sleep would be uninterrupted. And if the noise did get to me, I could always head to the beach, where the ocean sound would drown out hammers and saws.

And of course, the thought of watching hot, muscled, shirtless contractors made my breath catch in my throat.

There was a light on inside the house, but I didn't see any movement. Molly tugged gently, reminding me that we weren't out here to snoop on our neighbors. "But Molly, hot, shirtless contractors! Think about it!" I tried to convince her with a laugh. Molly merely looked up at me and wagged her tail. She apparently had more pressing issues. "Okay, okay, let's get strolling."

We returned to the house at dusk. The evening was cooling down, even after the heat of the day. I'd left all the windows open, and the breeze coming in felt nice against my skin. I walked around the living room, opening drawers and checking out the books on the shelves. There was lots of popular fiction by current authors and I knew I'd spend many a happy hour burning through those books.

An old rolltop desk held decks of cards, tons of jigsaw puzzles, and a modem and router for the wireless internet connection. Earlier I'd plugged in my laptop to charge it, so I grabbed it and settled myself on the living room couch with a cup of decaf coffee. Molly was sound asleep on the floor beside me, her feet twitching as she chased what I assume were squirrels in her dream. I logged on and checked email. Sixty-four unread emails awaited me. I sighed deeply. The Cell had been chatty today. Barb, Lisa, and I had been close friends for almost twenty years. The three of us were spread across the country and "met" online on a scrapbooking message board. Our friendship had grown on that message board, deepened with the next one, and solidified when we opened our own forum and gallery. We kept that going until Facebook changed the way everyone talked to each other. But we were still in constant daily contact and tried to see each other in person at least once a year. We referred to ourselves as the Cell. I forget now how that exactly happened, but it had something to do with the idea that three of us separated were worthless, but together we equaled one entire brain cell. That got shortened to "Cell" years ago.

Dashing off a quick message, I let them know I was settled in and a little about the house. We had plans for the two of them to spend a week with me in July. It took me almost thirty minutes to catch up on Cell-Mail. With a glance at the clock, I decided one more cup of coffee wouldn't kill me. "It may not kill you," I said out loud. "But you'll be up peeing at two a.m."

I quickly shushed myself and poured water into my coffee maker.

I carried my mug to the glassed-in front porch, shutting off the lights inside the house on my way. The chair I chose faced the ocean and I settled in. The night was quiet except for the crashing waves. With not a soul around, the evening was calm and serene and lit only by the full moon hanging low in the sky. I sat there sipping my coffee and thought about my day, reminding myself of all the things that needed to be added to my gratitude journal before going to sleep. I'd started this practice a few years ago and found it a wonderful way to go to sleep. Now I recommended it to all my friends who needed a mood boost. I took a quick moment to jot down three things I was grateful for today: the sound of the waves, coffee, and serenity. Immediately I felt a lift in my mindset. There were days when the only thing I could think of were comfortable shoes and unsmudged eyeliner, but hey, gratitude was gratitude.

I heard Molly before I saw her, stretching and coming to find me. "In here, girl," I whispered, not wanting to break the silence of this exquisite night. She lay back down near my feet and was almost asleep, when suddenly her large head lifted and her ears moved forward on alert. A small woof escaped her throat and she stood up and stared out the window toward the house next door. Her tail started waving back and forth, which meant friend, not foe. Whatever Molly sensed had not become apparent yet to me, until I saw the front door open next door and out came the biggest, most solid-looking bulldog I'd ever laid eyes on. He had huge jowls, and his jutting underbite made me want to get in there with some dental tools to fix his teeth.

The bulldog waddled to the edge of the front patio and lifted his leg. When he was done marking his territory, he walked over to the edge of the patio nearest my porch, stood stock-still, and stared right at me.

Startled, I stifled a laugh. The bulldog seemed to look at me, but that was impossible. The porch was dark, and the moon hadn't yet risen high enough to create shadows. Molly's snuffle and tail thump made me realize that the bulldog wasn't sensing me as much as he had picked up the scent of my dog.

The door behind him swung open and a man walked out. It was almost impossible to see his features, but he appeared tall and his hair looked dark. I couldn't tell you if he was twenty-five or sixty-five.

"Tank, what are you doing over there?" I heard the deep timbre of his voice say. Funny how we dog people ask questions of our pets like they are going to answer us. As if Tank was going to turn around and say, "Why, it appears we have new neighbors and apparently they have a dog also. I'm hoping for an invitation inside and a butt sniff." Again, I stifled a laugh that came out as a choked cough. There were probably a good thirty feet between where I sat and where the man and his dog stood. With all the windows open, my combined giggle and cough traveled easily to their ears. Molly chose that moment to bark.

The man straightened up and looked at my porch. I wasn't sure if I should call out a greeting or sit quietly. Since I wasn't dressed, my hair was still caught up in a messy bun , and I hadn't looked in a mirror in hours, I chose the sit quietly option.

After a moment, the man turned to go back into his house, calling Tank, who waddled behind him and went inside. Exhaling, I immediately wondered about my neighbors. Renters? Owners? Married? Children? I sat there a while longer until I yawned so wide my jaw popped. Rubbing the side of my face, I stood and carried my mug to the sink. I let Molly out for one last potty trip and after she was done I walked through the house closing windows and made sure the doors were locked.

As I started to close the last window on the porch, the strains of one of my favorite songs reached my ears. I couldn't tell where it was coming from, but it had to be close. I guessed it was Tank's daddy spinning some tunes and I stood for quite a while listening to the eclectic variety of music.

Soon I found myself swaying to the beat of one great song after another, then shimmying around the porch shaking what my mama gave me. I closed my eyes, twirled around, and waved my arms out wide. Mid-twirl I heard a noise outside that snapped my eyes open. Slightly dizzy from my last spin, I found myself looking right at my neighbor. And Tank. Tank wasn't watching me, but his owner most definitely was. I looked down and saw my disheveled appearance all too clearly in the moonlight. My eyes traveled from my bare feet, baggy running shorts, tight tank top, no bra—*OH MY GOD no bra*—and back to my neighbor. Though I couldn't make out the details of his face, I knew he was grinning. And then, inch by inch, I backed out of the porch, into the living room, and ran upstairs where Molly—that traitor!—had already claimed half my bed.

I flopped down next to her and she seemed to grin. "Yeah, very funny," I said, burying my burning face in her soft coat. "I will never be able to face this guy." I knew what I must have looked like: a hot mess spinning all over the porch with no bra! I groaned again, my entire body blushing at the thought.

Sighing deeply, I chalked this up to yet another day in the life of Sara Maloney. I crawled under the covers and pushed Molly over onto her side of the bed. The Cell would get a kick out of this story and I imagined the morning email. As I dozed off, I thought about the guy next door, and my dreams that night were filled with music, dancing, and bulldogs.

CHAPTER 2

It was barely dawn when I opened my eyes the next morning to the sight of Molly's big brown eyes mere inches from face. The sun's early rays filtered in through my bedroom window, and I stretched and yawned. Happy to see me awake, she licked my cheek and wagged her tail. I ruffled her feathery ear fur and contemplated the day ahead.

Deciding I'd let the weather dictate my agenda, I flipped on the bedroom TV. I wasn't a big fan of the tube but enjoyed some sitcoms and one or two reality shows. The local weather station promised another hot sunny day. Molly padded downstairs while I used the bathroom. After showering quickly and brushing my teeth, I joined her downstairs and let her out for a quick tinkle. Back inside, I made coffee and took it upstairs with me, sipping it while I put some makeup on and blow-dried my hair.

I looked down at what I'd thrown on to take Molly out and decided it would do just fine for the morning. Long shorts and another tank top, *with* a bra this time. I was already quite tan, thanks to some warm May weekends spent on my small deck at home. I spread sunscreen on my arms and legs, remembering to do the tops of my feet. You only forget to do that once. By this time, the sun was rising in the sky and the air was already warm.

Back downstairs, I poured another cup of coffee and a bowl of cereal. Molly was happily inhaling her kibble, looking up every so often to see if I might share any shredded wheat with her. "Dream on, Fur Face," I said. "Your kibble probably tastes better than this, anyway."

After breakfast I booted up the laptop. Forty-five unread emails. "Seriously? Are you kidding me? I never want to hear that I'm the chatty one." I typed my story from the night before and while I was waiting for the Cell's reaction, I caught up on the emails, responded to what needed responding to, and deleted what didn't. As expected, my friends were laughing hysterically at my escapade with my neighbor.

Speaking of neighbors, I peeked out the porch window but didn't see a soul stirring. *Maybe he's not an early riser like me.* Molly bumped my knee with her nose. "Ready for a stroll?" I cocked my head at her. Filling my travel mug with coffee—have I mentioned I love coffee?—and with Molly happy on her leash, we started down the front walk. The boards were empty: a few joggers and a young mommy pushing a stroller. It was almost exactly one mile to the north end where the boards ended. The sun warmed the air and I realized today would be a beach day no matter what. Perhaps I'd start out in the front of the house and move down to the ocean this afternoon.

Back at the house, Molly drank some water and sprawled

out in the living room, asleep before the last of her fur hit the carpet. I ran upstairs and changed into my bathing suit, a daring black bikini. I'd checked myself out from all angles in the store before purchasing it and two others like it in different colors. My body wasn't bad for an old broad. I was short but still slender and sported some pretty large tatas. Of course, those tatas were no longer sitting as high on my chest anymore, but with the right foundation, nobody would ever know that.

I pulled my long hair up into a bun and grabbed my beach towel. On my way through the living room, I grabbed one of the bestsellers from the bookshelf and headed outside. I settled myself on a beach chair and read for about thirty minutes. Every so often, I would glance over at the house next door, but it seemed deserted. No man, no dog, no contractors. *Weird. I wonder when the noise will start.*

Deciding it was time to tan my back, I spread my beach towel on the warm soft sand and kneeled on it. I mentioned my tatas, right? Well, there was an art to how I made this position comfortable. With my hands, I pushed the sand under the towel, making a gully for my tatas. Sometimes it took a few tries before getting the correct depth. Today was one of those days. I'd scoop, lie down, wiggle, sit up, scoop, lie down... you get the idea. As I tested the depth for the third time, I sensed, rather than saw, that I had an audience. I felt eyes watching me. In fact, I sensed multiple eyes.

I lay there very still for a moment, eyes closed, praying that when I opened them I would be alone. After a deep breath, I opened my eyes and slowly lifted my gaze... and looked directly into Tank's eyes. Tank seemed unimpressed but didn't break the stare. I let my eyes shift slightly to the left, where they landed on a pair of legs. Male legs. Very shapely, masculine, bare male legs. I let my eyes move up the legs. Nice torso. Cut-off blue jean shorts. T-shirt. Nice arms. This body did some weight lifting. The perfect amount of hair—not gorilla-like, but a nice manly fur.

Forcing my eyes to his face, I quickly closed them again. He was handsome, more than handsome. Handsome *and* hot. Thick dark hair fell loosely, slightly curly and wavy like he was a few weeks past due for a haircut. Blue eyes, thick lashes. He looked vaguely familiar, but I couldn't place him. This man who watched me dig holes for my boobs, this handsome, hot, well-built man, this man I was living right next door to, was desperately trying to hold in his laughter.

My face burned, yet I forced myself to meet his gaze. We both started to speak at the same time, but before any words could come out, his cell phone rang. Checking the caller ID, he frowned and quickly answered it. "Hello? Yes... what? When?" As his voice grew increasingly distressed, he turned away and went back into the house to continue his conversation.

Leaning my head back on my towel, I wasn't sure if I was relieved or sad. Relieved, I decided. Saved by the cell phone. Tank chose that moment to waddle off his patio and into the sand of my front yard, and soon I was eye level with his huge chest. That's when Tank kissed me and went back home.

Laughing, I rose to my knees, gathered my towel and book, and went inside my house. I could hear my neighbor on the phone, and he didn't sound happy. I let myself muse about all that a bit while I grabbed a bottle of water. The summer stretched ahead of me—and hopefully included this very hot man. If he could only get past my tata antics, we might be in business for some fun.

Oooh, naughty Sara, I thought. I'd been on a couple of dates since my divorce. One guy was a blind date set up by my friend Mary. I almost disowned her the next day and vowed to never go on a blind date again. Talk about brutal, I spent two long hours listening to this guy's mouth problems. Once he found out I had a dental background, he was in tooth heaven. At one point, he opened his mouth, stuck his finger in, and asked me my opinion on his recently placed crown. If that wasn't bad enough, prior to showing me his molars, he had consumed a handful of those yummy cheese crackers conveniently supplied by the bartender to make you thirsty.

My stomach roiled at the memory. I shook it off, finished my water, and decided to set up my makeshift studio. I was itchy to get inky and grungy. Though I hated destroying the perfection of the porch, it truly did have the best light. My only concern was the distraction of the boardwalk and dune.

Oh, who was I kidding? It wasn't the view I was thinking about. It was my hunky neighbor. I laughed at myself as I opened the boxes and set up my craft table. I filled my spinning organizer with scissors, sanding implements of every size and shape, my adhesive gun, and an endless supply of glue dots. Out came my markers and pencils, my inks, and some of my favorite stamps. As I organized and set up my area, I found myself smiling and humming one of the tunes from the night before. *He probably thinks you're a complete lunatic. He's probably hiding inside his house so he won't be witness to another spectacle.*

I pulled out a stack of canvases, all prepped and ready to go. A gallon of collage medium, along with paint and paper, and I was ready to create some art. Every so often I'd look next door, hoping for a glimpse of my next-door neighbor, but no one was stirring, not even Tank.

The rest of the afternoon passed without incident, and except for a couple of Tank sightings, my hot neighbor was MIA.

The next morning dawned cloudy and much cooler, and it looked like rain would be coming before long. After showering and applying some makeup, I pulled on an adorable pair of yoga pants and matching hoodie. A bun was the way to go—rain and my hair did not get along well.

Molly and I took a shorter walk than usual, although the weather would never deter Molly. Only a clap of thunder would have brought our walk to a screeching halt. Back at the house, I checked email, chatted with the Cell, and cleaned up the kitchen. As I was pouring my second cup of coffee, I heard a car door slam. A second slam soon followed. I checked the driveway but saw nothing that would indicate visitors.

The sound of Tank's bark made Molly run to a porch window to see if there was something she should be barking at. Knowing I was being nosy, yet not really caring, I stood near Molly and looked at the house next door. A white Mercedes was parked on the street next to my neighbor. A woman as stunning as the Mercedes was walking up the boards to his front door. She was tall, slender, poised, blond, and stunning. She walked with a confident air. Her mouth turned down into a slight frown as she carefully negotiated her way along the wooden walkway in high wedge sandals.

A younger version of the woman followed behind, without the confident walk. Pretty, yet sullen, and the unmistakable look of a rebellious teenager. *Ah, crap.* I frowned. *Wife. Kid. There goes my summer. No hot available man.* Of course, that thought was quickly wiped away when the woman knocked on his porch door. Knocking? A wife wouldn't be knocking. My spirits rose as the door opened and Hot Man gazed at the woman, a look of grim resignation on his handsome face.

Luckily enough for me, the porch window was open about five inches, allowing me to hear their conversation.

"Hello, Cynthia," he said coolly.

"Hello, Erik," was her response, every bit as cool if not cooler than his greeting.

His eyes lit up as he caught sight of the teenager sulking behind the woman. "Hi, sweetie, you okay?" he asked.

As hard as I tried, and trust me, I tried hard, I couldn't make out what the girl mumbled in return. Erik—I didn't have to call him Hot Man anymore; he finally had a name!—moved to the side and the two women entered the house. Before closing the door behind him, I caught a look of pure fear on his face.

Within a few moments, he reemerged from the house and walked toward the Mercedes. When he returned, he was pulling a large suitcase and his arms were filled with overnight bags and a backpack. I watched all this unfold while standing at my craft table, moving items from side to side and hoping to catch a glimpse of the people next door. This was almost as good as a reality show.

It didn't take long for more action to start. Within five minutes the woman exited the house, stalked back to her car, and drove off. The porch door flew open and the teenager came out and dropped into one of the patio chairs. She hung her head and stared at her feet. It didn't look like she was crying, but she certainly didn't look happy.

I watched her face for a few minutes, half expecting Erik to come out and talk to this clearly upset teenager. Every so often, I would look out the porch window to see if she was still there, and sure enough, there she sat… unmoving except for her feet, which kicked at the paving stones beneath them. Taking a huge breath, she let it out and her shoulders started to shake.

Ah, crap. She's crying. I hated seeing people cry. It bothered me to no end. I tried sending a mental message to Erik to come outside and comfort this young girl who I assumed was his daughter.

Apparently, Erik didn't have his radar on, because it was just me and a sobbing young woman, with a window and some sand separating us.

"C'mon, Molly, we're going out." Never one to ignore the word *out*, Molly padded onto the porch, her tail wagging.

I wasn't sure what I was going to do, but I knew I couldn't get any work done with someone who looked like her heart was breaking right in front of me. Snapping the leash on Molly's collar, I stepped out the front door, and true to myself, promptly fell down the two steps and into the sand.

I heard a muffled snicker and looked over at the girl. Even though tears were streaming down her face, there was a smile. *Well, fixed that.* Molly stood next to me, patiently waiting for me to stand, brush the sand from my butt, and proceed with the original plan of a walk.

As I brushed myself off, I grinned at the girl. "I'm a bit of a klutz, always doing something to embarrass myself." The girl smiled back at me and I was struck by how pretty she was even with a runny nose and streaky mascara.

Molly and I walked over to where she was sitting, and I stuck out my hand. "Hi. I'm Sara." The girl tentatively put her hand out and shook mine. "Danielle. But everyone calls me Dani." Her voice was still a bit shaky, but her grip was firm.

"It's nice to meet you, Dani," I said. "Sorry my first impression was so graceful."

Giggling, Dani's face transformed from the sullen angst of teenage hell to that of an adorable young woman. "S'okay," she said. "Made me laugh, but I'm sorry I laughed at you."

"S'okay," I responded. "Oh, and this is Molly."

"Hi, Molly," Dani said, patting Molly on the head. Molly didn't need any encouraging and moved closer so that Dani could reach her more easily. That made Dani giggle again. "Do you live here?" She nodded toward the Pendleton.

"I wish," I replied. "I'm here for the summer though, through September actually. How about you?"

Dani waved her hand carelessly at the house. "Oh, this is my dad's place. He bought it about a month ago and he's remodeling it. He said he needed a beach house because the book he's writing is set at the beach and he had to be 'in the beach mindset.'"

I nodded like I knew what she was talking about. I wasn't sure what I wanted clarification on first. "I haven't actually met your dad yet," I said. "He's a writer? Has he written anything I might know?"

"I dunno. I guess he's kind of famous. He's had a few bestsellers. *New York Times* list and stuff. His name is Erik Hanson."

Erik Hanson. Kind of famous? Ha. He was more than that; he was one of the most popular fiction writers in the literary world today. One of his novels was on the bookshelf inside the Pendleton. I'd not had the pleasure of reading this newer novel yet, but I certainly knew who he was. It also explained why he looked familiar.

"He's just come back from Europe," Dani continued, twirling her hair in her fingers. "He was on a book tour."

I nodded, hoping she'd continue and I'd learn more about her father. Suddenly her hands flew to her face, apparently remembering that she had been crying not five minutes earlier. She swiped at her eyes, wiping at the black streaks and succeeded in making them even streakier. "Crap," she muttered. "Ruined my fu… freaking makeup."

Before I could say a word, she stood and started for the house. She turned toward me as she opened the door. "I guess I'll see you around. Maybe we could walk dogs together. My dad has a bulldog named Tank."

I didn't get a chance to tell Dani that Tank and I were old friends. As if on cue, Tank poked his big head out the door. Molly wagged her tail. Tank drooled a bit and went back inside. Dani closed the door behind her. Looking down at Molly, I said, "Well, that was interesting. We learned a little, didn't we?"

Molly stood up, ready to get on with business. I ruffled her ears and we took a good long walk. As soon as we returned to the Pendleton, the sky opened and it started to pour. The rest of the afternoon and evening passed uneventfully.

After emailing the Cell with the neighbor update, I ate dinner and settled in for the night, coffee in hand. I glanced at the bookshelf and my hand reached out and grabbed Erik Hanson's book almost of its own accord. Quickly I turned to the back flyleaf. *Yep, that's him.* I stared down into that incredibly handsome face. The picture was of Erik leaning against a weathered doorjamb, his arms crossed and a small smile on his face. He was dressed in jeans and a flannel shirt, and work boots completed the outfit.

I read the short bio under the photograph.

The Sin of Omission is Erik Hanson's fourth novel. The writer travels between his homes in Prescott, Arizona and Lake George, New York.

Damn it, I thought. Nothing about a wife or ex-wife. I sighed, finished my coffee, and turned in for the night.

CHAPTER 3

At some point during the night, a thunderstorm rolled in and I awoke to a seventy-five-pound golden retriever on my head. Seventy-five pounds of shivering fur. I patted Molly and soothed her, but it was almost an hour before she was calm enough to fall back to sleep. A glance at the clock told me it was 4:00 a.m. Yawning, I stretched, glanced at Molly, now sound asleep, and got up. I was done for the night.

After making coffee, I carried the steaming mug to the porch. I looked up at the moon, visible now that the storm had pushed through. Daybreak was still a couple of hours away. The coffee energized me, and I worked on straightening my craft area.

One thing led to another, and before long I was dusting the main floor and wiping down the bathroom. I pulled out the vacuum and by the time I was done, I had vacuumed up enough fur to cover another golden retriever. "It's a wonder she's not bald," I muttered, dumping the canister contents into the trash. Tying up the garbage bag, I opened the back door and walked across the driveway to the garbage cans.

The sun was coming up and the sky was clear. I sniffed the sea air and once again counted my blessings. Yet when I reached the back door, I stopped counting those blessings: it had shut behind me and locked me out.

Don't panic. I did anyway. *Crap, crap, crap.*

I took a quick inventory of my situation. It was around 6:30 a.m. I was wearing my pajamas, which consisted of a tank top and panties. There was, of course, no bra. I sighed and wondered if perhaps I ought to wear a bra 24/7 just in case. I was barefoot, unshowered, and sweaty from housecleaning. Hell, I had dog hair between my toes. No key on me, my dog was inside, my house was locked tight, and I had to pee.

I sat down on the back step. "Figure it out, Sara, just figure it out. There's got to be *some* way to get in without breaking a window." I snapped my fingers. *The porch window!* I'd opened it while cleaning. *If I can somehow pop the screen, I can climb in that way.*

Practically running to the front of the house, I looked up at the window. If I stood on my tippy toes, I could reach the bottom sill, but barely. I glanced around. My beach chairs were the lowboy type and wouldn't do me any good. *There might be a ladder in the garage.* As I turned to go back, I noticed the step ladder in front of Erik's house. I scanned the area. Nobody was moving around, and his house was dark. I tiptoed—why was I tiptoeing?—to the ladder and carried it back the ten feet to the side of my porch. I set it up and anchored it as best I could in the soft sand. Climbing up a few rungs, I examined the screen. I pushed and tugged and decided a full-frontal attack would be necessary. If I wrecked the screen, so be it. It was cheaper than glass to replace.

I gave the screen a push. Nothing. I gave it a harder shove. The screen didn't budge, but the ladder did, and suddenly, I found myself on my back in the sand.

This is getting old, I thought. I set the ladder back up and climbed up once again. This time, I didn't take any guff from the screen and punched it right off its tracks.

"Success!" I cried, and quickly clapped my hand over my mouth, shushing myself.

I crawled over the windowsill and teetered for a moment, my butt in the air. As I grunted and pulled one of my legs over the sill, I heard a man's voice.

"Is everything okay? Do you need help?"

Oh GOD no. Oh, please don't be him.

"I'm okay." I gasped, blood rushing to my head as I swung half in and half out of my porch window. "Just fine, thank you."

Whoever it was, he was getting a bird's eye view of my butt, but I tried not to think about that. I managed to pull my second leg through and dropped down onto my worktable below the window. Lying there for a brief moment, I considered the options before me.

I could stand up and wave happily at whoever the voice belonged to. Or, I could slide to the floor, and slink my way into the living room, ignoring the man outside.

Rising slowly, I peeked over the windowsill and into the blue eyes of Erik Hanson.

"H-h-h-hi," I said, totally feeling like an idiot. "I locked myself out and I borrowed your ladder and I'm sorry and thanks, but I'm inside now and fine and I'll bring your ladder back as soon as I'm dressed," I babbled.

Luckily, all he could see of me was the top of my head and my eyes.

"No worries. Glad it was there. I'll bring it back myself," he said. "You sure you're okay?"

"Fine. I'm fine," I said. "Thanks. Have a good day." And with that, I took option B and crawled into the living room.

Molly, aroused by the racket of me breaking in, stood in the living room smiling at me, wagging her tail. "Fine watchdog you are," I grumbled.

Molly simply watched me as I stalked across the room and went upstairs to shower. Screen replacement would have to wait. He might still be out there.

Once I was showered, made up, hair done, and dressed, I reappeared on the porch. I looked around outside but saw no one. Luckily, I hadn't done much, if any, damage and was able to pop the screen back into place from the inside.

I took Molly for a quick walk and when I returned, I spent a few hours on the porch working on a canvas. At one point, I looked up and spotted Dani coming outside to take Tank for a walk. The sullen look was still there but not as bad as the day before.

When I waved at her as she came back, she smiled tentatively. "What are you doing?" she asked through the window.

"I'm an artist," I answered. "I set up the porch as my studio. Would you like to see?"

"Sure!" she exclaimed, her eyes lighting up. "Can I bring Tank?"

"Absolutely," I replied. "The more the merrier."

I held the door open as Dani and Tank entered the porch, Dani wiping her feet on the mat inside the door. Tank wasn't quite so polite—his sand-covered paws messed up the floor.

"Oooh, I'm sorry!" Dani exclaimed, her eyes widening at the sandy mess.

"Don't worry about it," I said. "Do you have any idea how much sand Molly drags in here every day? It's all part of beach living."

"I guess I'll get used to it." She glanced down at her legs and feet, glaringly white, toenails showing the remnants of an old pedicure. Her gaze moved to my tanned legs and hot pink toenails and her teeth caught her bottom lip. "I like your polish."

"Thanks! It's called Hot Pinky Toe and you can borrow it if you'd like."

Dani's face lit up and her toes wiggled in anticipation. "That would be great!" she exclaimed. "Thanks!"

Turning every which way, she looked around my makeshift studio. Her eyes roamed over my supplies: paintbrushes in a cup of water, a gallon jug of collage medium, canvases stacked in the corner… and when her eyes fell on my half-completed canvas in the middle of the table, her fingers tentatively reached toward it but didn't quite touch the edge.

"You can touch it," I said. "It's dry."

Her fingers flew back to it, traveling over all the textures and colors. Lifting it, she brought the canvas close to her face. "How do you do this?" she asked, her eyes never leaving the surface of the mixed-media piece.

"Well, I build it in layers using all kinds of cool stuff, cover it all in collage medium, and voilà!"

"Cool. Can I watch you work sometime?"

I laughed. "Sure. I don't know how exciting that will be for you, but you can certainly watch me. In fact, I'll show you how and you can create your own canvas."

Satisfied and smiling, Dani turned her attention to Molly, who was standing stock-still in the entryway to the living room, nose to nose with Tank. "Molly meet Tank. Tank meet Molly." She giggled.

The two dogs eyeballed each other, Molly's huge tail wagging, Tank's butt wiggling as if there were a tail there. After a moment, and an obligatory butt sniff, the two dogs padded off to the kitchen to check out food possibilities.

Dani and I smiled at each other and I was happy to see that her face was washed clean and she hadn't caked on the eye makeup like the day before. She was a gorgeous young woman and I could see a resemblance to her father. Her long blond hair was caught up in a messy bun like mine. I looked at the clock and noticed it was past lunchtime.

"Hungry?" I asked. "We could take a walk down to the QuikMart and grab a sandwich or something." I mentally crossed my fingers that she would say yes. I was feeling so drawn to this young woman—memories of my own teenage angst sprang fresh to my mind.

Her eyes lit up. "Really? Sure!" Then her face fell. "But let me go ask my dad first, okay?" She whistled for Tank, hooked on his leash, and skipped back over to the house next door. Two minutes later she was back sans Tank, a few dollar bills crumpled in her hand.

"Dad was writing so he didn't care. He gave me some money for lunch."

We both looked down at the wad of bills in her hand. What I thought were dollar bills were actually three twenties.

"Did you tell your dad we were going to QuikMart? I think the most expensive item in the store is four ninety-five," I said with a grin.

With a giggle, she tossed her head. "This is what my dad does. He gives me money because he feels guilty."

I looked at her closely. "What makes you think that?"

"My mom said so. She said that he's trying to make up for not being there."

Her face started to close down, and I wasn't about to let that happen. "Hey," I said, "let's talk more about this on our way to the store. My stomach is growling, and I heard yours from next door."

She laughed, the gloom of the previous moment gone.

We chatted as we walked the short block and Dani told me more about her parents' divorce. "It happened when I was four," she said. "My mom said she got tired of always being alone. Dad was gone on book tours all the time, and when he did come home, he was in his office writing."

"That had to be very hard on her," I said, feeling a bit of compassion for that cold, hard-looking woman I'd caught sight of yesterday.

"Well," Dani continued, "Dad said he was just trying to take care of the family and did what he had to do."

I could see the girl was torn between her parents. "How often do you see your father?"

"He gets me every other weekend when he's not traveling, and the holidays alternate. But my mom's boyfriend surprised her yesterday morning with a world cruise, and she decided my dad could have me for the entire summer. She knew he'd be here writing and not traveling." A frown touched her lips. "I don't think he's very happy I'm here."

I reached out and touched her arm. "I'm sure he's thrilled. He's probably just a bit unsure of himself with you."

We had reached the QuikMart at this point and we pushed the glass door open into the frigidly air-conditioned store. After ordering a couple of turkey subs, we checked out the cosmetics aisle while they were being made.

Dani squealed when her eyes fell on the same hot pink nail polish I had on my toes. "Look, Sara! It's Hot Pinky Toe!" She grabbed the bottle. "Now I don't have to borrow yours!"

She also picked up a package of silver toe rings and some nail polish remover. I smiled at her. "I see a pedicure in somebody's future."

Someone called out our number at the deli counter, signaling that our sandwiches were ready. Dani insisted on paying for my sandwich, and considering the amount of money her father had allotted for lunch, I thanked her and accepted the offer.

We chatted about this and that on the walk back and I found myself truly liking her and looking forward to her company over the summer. Plus, it could give me the chance to get to know her hunky dad better.

Molly was happy to see us return. "You are a spoiled rotten

girl." I laughed at her. "You know you'll get some sandwich and I haven't even unwrapped it yet."

After lunch, Dani returned home with promises of an early morning dog walk the next day. I laughed to myself, thinking that "early" to a sixteen-year-old was probably noon. The late afternoon sun was warm and there wasn't a cloud in the sky, so I decided to take Molly to the beach for a romp in the ocean. Since it was still off-season, the "no dog" rule wasn't enforced.

I changed into my bathing suit—a cute red bikini—and grabbed a towel, a couple of rubber balls, and Molly's leash. "Let's go swimming, girl!"

Molly danced around so much I almost couldn't get her leash hooked. She knew she was in for a treat. I wrapped the towel around me as a cover-up, gave Molly one of the balls to hold in her mouth, and we walked down the beach to the water's edge. It was low tide and the water was calm and warm. The beach was virtually empty, only a few people walking and a couple of fishermen. Dropping the towel, I headed into the water with Molly. I tossed one of the balls and she jumped into a wave to get it. We played for a while, me tossing, Molly catching, until we both grew tired and I got sweaty. I jumped into a wave to cool off, and as I came up out of the water, I saw Molly bounding out of the ocean and running up the sand.

"Molly!" I yelled. "Stop! Stay."

Molly turned to look at me, tail wagging, spraying water all around her. She was giving me her golden smile, and then I saw why.

Erik and Tank were walking along the water's edge. I stood frozen in the water, knowing without a shadow of a doubt what was going to happen next.

Sure enough, and as if in slow motion, I watched as Molly ran up to Tank, and after a quick greeting, turned her full attention to Erik. Standing up on her hind legs, she rested her soaking wet, sandy paws on Erik's chest, knocking him flat on his extremely cute butt. Sandy kisses followed, and, in short order, Erik was covered in seawater, sand, and dog slobber. Tank sat back on his haunches and watched the action unfold.

I stood there, knee-deep in the ocean, my mouth open and in too much shock to utter one word. Erik somehow sat up, which for some reason made my normally mellow golden even more excited. Molly started to wag her tail and dance around, spraying droplets of water everywhere.

"Molly!" I managed to squeak out. "Stop, sit, stay!"

As if her conniption never happened, Molly stopped, sat, and stayed, but kept smiling at Erik. I saw Erik grin back at her and then look over at me. His lips moved from an upturn to a big O and his eyes opened wide. Before he could call out a warning, I was hit from behind by a wave and pushed face-first underwater.

Caught off guard, I tumbled in the wave, slammed bottom, rolled around a bit, and was finally able to push myself up out of the water. Choking a bit and wiping stinging salt water from my eyes, I dragged myself from the water and trudged toward the two dogs and Erik. There was no point trying to make believe that didn't just happen. Once again, Erik saw me at my best—elegant and graceful I was not.

I couldn't believe our very first words to each other were about to be spoken, and we were both soaked and sandy.

"I am *so* sorry Molly did that," I said, my eyes traveling

over this gorgeous man. "She's *never* done that before. I don't know what came over her!"

Erik looked down at Molly and back to me. His eyes traveled slowly from my hair, which I'm sure was a complete wreck, down to my mouth, and then quickly dropped back to Molly.

"Um… I'm not sure how to tell you this…" he stammered and pointed in the general area of my chest.

I looked down and to my horror saw that one entire boob was completely out of the bikini top. I was standing three feet from Erik with my left tata swinging in the breeze. *This kind of crap only happens to me. I'm convinced of it.*

Very slowly, without making eye contact, I reached up, pulled out my suit top, and dropped the offending tata back where it belonged.

"Okay then," I said, my face a deep purple. "I guess this is where I make believe this never happened. This, and the window incident and the sand-digging incident."

I stuck out my sandy hand. "Hi. My name is Sara. It's nice to finally meet you."

Erik's face was a study in emotions. He seemed unsure what to do, his face revealing his struggle between laughter and fear.

He took my hand, his even sandier than mine, and shook it solemnly. "Hi, Sara. I'm Erik. It's… a pleasure."

Molly looked at us both and wagged her tail. "Yeah, this is all your doing, and you are totally enjoying yourself, aren't you?" I asked her.

"Again, I am *so* sorry about this. Molly has never done anything like that before. You must be soaked. I hope she didn't ruin anything." I managed to meet his eyes and Erik smiled at me.

"No worries. I'm fine. The sand made a soft cushion. A shower will fix the rest," he said, wiping his hands on his shorts. Since his shorts were even sandier, that didn't do him much good, and he gazed down at them with a perplexed look. "I guess I'd better head home."

As he turned to leave, an idea struck me, and I stopped him. "Erik, wait. I was wondering if you and Dani would like to join me one evening for dinner… just burgers on the grill or something?"

"I'd like that," he said. "You and Dani have become fast friends, haven't you?"

"Yes… she's a great kid. I've enjoyed the time we've spent together so far, and I'm looking forward to getting to know her better this summer."

Well, it's not just Dani I'd like to know better.

"So, okay," I said. "I'll let you know what night."

Erik smiled and saluted me, leading Tank up to the boards and back to his house. Molly and I headed directly to my outdoor shower. I hosed her off under the spray and clipped her leash to the outside line, letting her shake and roll in the shady driveway.

I showered off the salt, sand, and Molly's fur and we went inside to relax. After cooking dinner—yes, I consider nuking a frozen meal cooking—I caught up with the Cell. As expected, the new chapter in "How to meet a man by embarrassing yourself" greatly amused them.

Around 8:00 p.m. I called Molly and we walked the boards for a while, enjoying the warm, still bright evening. As I approached the Pendleton, I noticed Dani on her patio looking up and down the boardwalk.

"Scoping out cute guys?" I asked. "It's too early in the season yet. Wait a few weeks and you'll have dozens to choose from."

She laughed. "No, I was waiting for you to come back. My dad said he finally met you this afternoon."

I felt my face grow hot. "He did, did he? What did he say exactly?"

"Oh, he said Molly knocked him down and you invited us to dinner."

Phew. No mention of tatas.

"Want to help me decide which night and what the menu will be?" I asked.

"Awesome. Can we go to your house? I've got cabin fever here."

We were settled in the living room, me in a chair with my coffee, pen, and paper, Dani cross-legged on the floor with a bottle of water. Dani was absentmindedly scratching Molly behind the ears. Molly gazed at Dani with pure love.

Funny how you get an idea in your head about how something is going to be—this scenario never played into that idea, but now I was enjoying it immensely.

"Okay. Tomorrow's forecast is hot and sunny. How's that sound?"

"Cool," Dani responded. "Dad said we had nothing planned all week, so it should be fine."

"Now, menu. Do you guys like burgers?"

"Yep. Dad likes his with cheese, but I only like ketchup and pickles on mine."

"Potato or pasta salad?"

"Pasta. Dad likes that. He says potato salad gags him."

"Glad I asked." I laughed. "How about tomatoes? You guys like tomatoes?"

Dani wrinkled her nose. "Dad does. Not me. No taste."

"No taste? Seriously? A fresh warm Jersey tomato with salt and pepper?" I could practically taste it.

The nose wrinkled again.

I laughed. "No tomato for Dani. Check. What about drinks? Soda? Water? Lemonade? Iced tea?"

"Iced tea for me, please. Dad likes water or coffee. Oh, and he loves lemonade."

"What about beer or wine?" I asked.

"Nope. Dad doesn't drink." Her voice dropped. "Don't tell him I told you, but he's a recovering alcoholic."

She looked at me, eyes wide, as if I were going to drop judgment on her or her father.

"That's fantastic!" I said. "My brother is also. How long has your dad been in recovery?"

"Seventeen years. He stopped when mom got pregnant with me. He tried to do it on his own, but it was too hard, and he goes to meetings and has a sponsor and all that."

"You must be very proud of him."

"I guess…" she said. "Mom said she was really glad he got help."

"I know the feeling," I said, remembering what my brother was like before finding AA five years ago.

"So the menu is planned, and tomorrow I'll shop for everything," I said, writing out the grocery list.

Dani bit her lip. "Can I help?" She quickly added, "Only if you don't mind. Dad said I shouldn't bug you all the time."

I laughed. "Sure, you can help. I hate grocery shopping—it will be more fun with company. Let's plan on ten a.m. Meet me in my driveway and we'll go, okay?"

Dani jumped up from the floor. Oh, to be sixteen again—it would have taken me ten minutes to get up from that position, and another ten to stop limping. "Cool! I'll see you in the morning!"

After Dani left, I made one more cup of coffee and watched some mindless TV. I whistled for Molly around ten and said, "C'mon, my friend. Let's go for a walk."

Always ready to oblige, Molly smiled at me as she headed for the porch. I clipped on her leash and we headed for the boardwalk. Back inside a few minutes later, I changed into my comfy sleeping attire, which consisted of yoga shorts and a tank top, washed my face, and brushed my teeth.

I ran downstairs to make sure I'd locked up and as I moved toward the porch, I noticed a shadowy figure outside the door.

Startled, I grabbed the first weapon I could find. Okay, so a paintbrush wasn't the most dangerous item, and maybe it wouldn't instill fear in the eyes of my intruder, but if aimed well, I could probably shove it up a nostril.

At the same moment that I realized the porch was lit, and I was, as usual, braless, I also realized it was Erik outside my door, his hand raised as if to knock. Sighing with relief, and extremely thankful I hadn't attacked his nostril with my brush, I opened the door.

I stood with my arms crossed, hoping to disguise the whole braless thing I had going on.

"Hey," Erik said. "I'm sorry to come over so late. I saw the lights still on and figured you were still up."

"I was just heading to bed when I saw your shadow." I glanced down at my hand, which was still gripped around the paintbrush handle.

Erik's eyes followed mine, and his right eyebrow rose in question. "Were you painting or was that meant for my eyeball?"

Damn it. Eyeball. Much more lethal than the nostril.

I laughed and admitted it was my weapon of choice. "But it was your nostril that was in the gravest danger."

We stood for a moment in silence, Erik obviously with something on his mind and me just taking in the perfection of this man in front of me.

"Oh my gosh—where are my manners? Come in. Can I get you some coffee or something?" *Like a kiss or some heavy petting or third base?* I was pretty sure that last sentence was said only in my head.

"Coffee would be great. Black please," he replied, making his way into the living room.

I grabbed a hoodie that I had thrown on a chair earlier. Shrugging it on in the kitchen, I zipped it up and prayed it was enough camouflage. Once again, I pondered the logic of wearing a bra 24/7 around here.

Pouring Erik's coffee, and another for myself (was I daft?), I carried them carefully to the living room where he was sprawled on the couch, looking quite at home.

"Thanks." He glanced briefly at the hoodie. If I wasn't mistaken, a brief look of disappointment crossed his face, and this made me chuckle.

Lowering myself into the recliner next to the couch, I wrapped my hands around my coffee mug, propped my bare feet on the coffee table, and looked at Erik.

He raised his eyes from his mug. Once again, I was struck by his looks. My heart beat a little faster and I wasn't sure if that was because of this incredible specimen of man sitting three feet away or the caffeine going through my system.

Erik cleared his throat. "It's funny. I feel like I know you already."

I blushed. "Well, you've seen me do some amazingly embarrassing things, so of course you do."

"No, no, I mean Dani does nothing but talk about you, so I feel like I'm getting to know you through her eyes."

I laughed and tucked my legs underneath me. "Phew. I thought perhaps you were going to bring up the bathing suit fiasco."

Erik had the good sense to blush and not say a word. "So, big picnic tomorrow, huh?"

"Yep. Dani will help me shop and we'll plan on eating around five. Sound good?"

"Sounds good." He looked down at his coffee cup like he'd never seen one before. A puzzled look crossed his face and I could almost see him putting words together in his brain, forming sentences that would eventually be spoken. A subtle shake of his head told me he'd changed his mind about whatever he'd wanted to say.

Instead he cleared his throat again, put his cup on the table, and looked into my eyes. "I really appreciate all the time you're spending with Dani. She's taken to you."

More throat clearing.

"Promise me if she gets to be a pain in the ass you'll let me know."

Smiling at Erik, I assured him I was enjoying her company. "I promise, though."

"So, tell me about yourself," he said. "I can see you're into some type of art. What do you make?"

"Besides a mess?" I laughed. "I'm mostly into mixed media."

I watched that puzzled look cross his face again. *God he's cute.* My mind started to wander… and it wandered all over his cute face, masculine yet boyish, and proceeded down his neck, and I briefly wondered what it would feel like beneath my lips.

"Sara? Did you hear me?"

My eyes flew back up to Erik's questioning ones. "What? Huh? What did you say?" I stammered.

"I asked you what mixed media was." And then he gave me a Cheshire Cat smile. Damn it. He knew exactly where my mind had gone.

"Well, mixed media simply means using two or more different types of product to create something. For instance, I'll take a canvas, cover it with some paper, like pages from an old book, then some paint, maybe some watercolor crayons… layer after layer. You get the idea."

"I get the idea. Can I see your pieces?" The edges of his lips curved up.

My eyes widened, remembering all too well that he'd already seen a few of my very naked pieces. At least he had the good sense to blush.

"Walk this way," I said, making sure I swayed my hips a bit as he followed me to the porch.

After showing him some of my newly completed canvases and hearing some very sexy oohs and aahs—I'm pretty sure most of them came from *his* mouth—we walked back into the living room.

"So what else?" he asked. "What makes you… YOU?"

I thought about that question for a moment, chewing my lip and twirling a hunk of my hair. "I think my art defines me more than anything else in my life at the moment. I spent a lot of years doing the nine-to-five thing, doing the wife thing, doing the 'normal' thing." I crooked my index fingers as I said normal. "Now I'm doing twenty-four seven 'anything.' I am no longer a wife or an employee, nor do I ever plan on doing that again."

Watching as Erik's right eyebrow raised just a hair, I wondered if that reaction was to the wife part or the employee part. "This summer is meant to restore," I continued. "I promised myself I would take these four months to find out who I am and what I'm going to be when I grow up."

Stopping suddenly, I wondered why I was telling him all that. He was looking for info, not my dreams. We sat there in silence for a moment, watching each other. Although I had enough caffeine in my system to keep an elephant awake, I still stifled a yawn.

Erik stood quickly. "Hey, thanks for the coffee and the talk… and for not shoving the paintbrush up my nostril."

He lightly touched my chin with his fingertips, tipping my face up as if to kiss me. I closed my eyes, waiting for his lips to touch mine. After a few seconds of no other contact, I squinted open my eyes and stared into Erik's twinkling ones.

"Good night, Sara… see you tomorrow. Five p.m. How about I bring dessert?"

"Sure. Dessert. Sure," I stammered a bit, hoping he didn't think I was waiting for a kiss, even though I obviously was. Was I ever *not* going to embarrass myself in front of this man?

CHAPTER 4

I slept surprisingly well that night, although my dreams were filled with Erik, and I awoke to sunlight glinting off the ocean and the sound of hammering.

Rolling out of bed, I peeked through the shade at the house next door. Erik was on a ladder, hammer in hand, and I watched him for a few moments, admiring his build, enjoying how the muscles in his arms—nicely shown in his white T-shirt—moved and flexed with each strike.

I took a deep breath and stepped away from the window, knowing I could stand there all morning watching him. A quick look at the clock told me it was after eight already. When I glanced at my bed, Molly was still snoring. "Hey, lazy dog… we both slept in today, eh?"

Molly opened one eye, gave me half a dog smile, and stretched and yawned. Since she didn't look like she was in any hurry to get up, I took that opportunity to shower quickly. Throwing on my shorts and a tank top, I quickly swiped mascara on my lashes and pulled my wet hair back into a ponytail. I slid my toes into flip-flops and whistled at the lump of fur curled up on the bed.

The heat of the morning sun hit me as I opened the porch door and Molly and I stepped outside. Erik waved his hammer at us as we walked by. "I hope I didn't wake you with this," he called out.

"Oh no, I've been up," I lied. "I'm an early riser." *Yeah. Except for when I'm dreaming about YOU all night.*

Grinning, he waved the hammer in response and went back to his chore.

At 10:00 a.m. on the nose, Dani knocked on the porch door.

"Good morning, Sunshine!" Tired teenage eyes looked back at me.

"Morning." Dani yawned in response. "I can't believe my dad was hammering like that so early."

I laughed and gave her a quick pat on the back.

"Buck up, Buttercup. It's too gorgeous to be sleeping anyway, unless you're on the beach, and I hope we'll both have a chance to do that later."

That garnered an eye roll and a sleepy grin from her. We headed for the garage and I backed the Beetle out to the road. Cranking up the satellite radio, we sang loudly to the latest Adele hit, giggling at our attempts to hit the high notes, the low notes, and, well, all the other notes also.

Between the two of us, we had the cart filled in record time, checked out, filled the back seat with bags, and headed back home.

Dani carried bags while I let Molly out for a quick potty run.

When we exited the porch, Erik was on his ladder again. His eyes met mine and a zing ran through my body from my stomach to my toes, and all the spots in between. I wondered if Erik experienced a zing. Did I make him think naughty things? Did he mentally undress me like I was doing to him? A flush ran through me when I remembered he'd already seen me in various stages of undress.

In the few brief moments it took for me to have those thoughts, Erik's face changed from intense and thoughtful to intense and grinning.

Damn it. That man knew exactly where my mind went. How did he *do* that? Or was my lust that easily readable?

Trying to cover my emotions, I waved at him, smiling like my mind was on seashells and saltwater taffy instead of his finely muscled back and tight rear end. I'm pretty sure I failed miserably.

Smiling in return, he rested his hammer on the roof and waved back at me. His wolfy grin reinforced how miserably I'd failed at hiding my very physical reaction to him.

With a sigh, I tugged on Molly's leash. She was too busy grinning at Tank, who was watching Molly from inside his front door.

"What the heck is going on around here?" I whispered to Molly. Her tail wagged in response and her smile widened.

"Five o clock, right?" Erik called. He was waggling the damn hammer again.

He needed to stop doing that. Until now, I'd never met a man who could make a hammer waggle look naughty.

"Yes. Five. Dani is inside right now helping me put the groceries away. I'd better go help before she thinks I deserted her."

Dani and I made quick work of the dinner preparations and before we knew it, we had made the salads, plattered the meat for burgers, and made a huge pitcher of lemonade. We agreed to meet out front in an hour for some sunbathing and trashy magazine reading.

Dani left, and I straightened the house a bit, set out some candles for later when it got dark... thinking perhaps a romantic setting might spur Erik's imagination a bit. After changing into my suit, I grabbed a bottle of water and headed outside.

Erik came around the corner of his house as I hit the first step. His eyes deepened as he took a long look at me. I'm guessing my eyes deepened a bit themselves.

"Hi," I murmured.

His face crinkled into a smile. "Hi yourself. Ready for later?"

Oh, you have *no* idea, I thought. "Yep! Ready as I can be," I answered. "Dani was a huge help. We're going to get a little sun. We have magazines. I made pasta salad. And some lemonade."

Stop babbling, Sara. Clench your teeth together and stop *talking.*

"Excellent. I love lemonade," Erik said, continuing his journey around the house. "See you later!"

At that moment, Dani came out of the house, bottle of water in one hand and a bottle of lotion in the other.

"Ready?" I asked.

"Ready. Are we staying here, or going to the water?"

Thinking I was already cranked up enough, I decided that going down to the water would be a better idea than sitting here watching Erik work.

Setting our towels down near where the waves were rolling in, we lotioned up and hit the sand. After an hour of sun, sand, salt water, and trashy magazine reading, we were tanned, gritty, sweaty, sticky, and filled with stories of alien babies, red carpet mishaps, and celebrity love triangles. Life was good.

We headed back up to shower and get ready for the picnic.

"That was excellent, Sara… thanks," Dani said with a smile.

"Thanks right back at you. I enjoyed that. We'll have lots of days like that in the coming months, I promise."

Tears filled Dani's eyes and she gave me a quick hug. "Thanks," she whispered and went inside.

I stood for a moment watching her disappear inside the house. "Who would have thought," I said to myself.

Back home, I let Molly out for a quick potty run and stripped off my suit. I think I moaned out loud as the water from the shower sluiced over my body, rinsing all the icks of the day down the drain. I lathered my hair with a fruity-smelling shampoo and my body with a spicy oriental body wash. I made a mental note to use unscented body lotion upon exiting the shower, lest I end up smelling like I just walked through Macy's.

I chose my outfit carefully.

Low-slung cargo shorts in a most excellent shade of olive green and a black tank top, low cut, but not to the point of obscene. After all, there would be a sixteen-year-old present for at least *some* of the evening.

My special addition to the outfit was a matching bra and thong in black lace. Black flip-flops completed the picture.

I brushed on some mascara and blow-dried my hair, breathing in deeply as the warm, fruity smell filled the air around me. I threw a few hot rollers in to give me some curl and bounce and headed downstairs.

Molly watched me as I walked to the kitchen. "What?" I asked her. "Never saw me look this good, eh?"

I laughed when Molly let out a soft chuffing noise in response.

I knew between the outfit, the golden tan, the smooth skin, and the peek of lace, Erik didn't stand a chance.

That was the thought that crossed my mind exactly thirty seconds before I dumped most of the pitcher of lemonade over the front of myself.

"Son of a bitch!" I yelled. "Damn it to hell!" I grabbed paper towels and tried to wipe myself down, once again a sticky mess.

"Everything okay in there?" asked an amused voice from outside my kitchen window.

Damn it. Erik.

"Fine. I'm fine," I called back. "Just a little lemonade mishap."

"No lemons were harmed, were they?" came the chuckled response.

Great. Witty repartee through a window. "Lemons are all safe, but I need to go unsticky myself and unsticky the kitchen floor, so if you will excuse me…"

Another chuckle was the only response and I heard his footsteps on the gravel outside. I stripped off my top and shorts at the landing to the lower level and tossed them down the back stairs to the general vicinity of the washing machine.

You know how they say timing is everything in life?

Erik chose that moment to walk past my back door. My glass back door. My glass back door with the shade that was not pulled down because it was daytime and normally people don't stand in front of their glass back doors with the shade not pulled down in their pretty black lace undies.

We both froze. I'd gotten enough sun today that I don't think my blush was visible, although I don't think Erik was looking at my face.

A slow smile spread across his face as his eyes traveled up and down my body. He put his hands on his hips and let out a long, low whistle.

"Wow," he called through the glass. "You never said it was a come-as-you-are picnic."

There was no way to get out of this gracefully. So I waved, spun around and ran to the safety of the kitchen… remembering too late that I was wearing a thong and Erik just got a full view of my butt.

Upstairs once again, I rinsed off, lotioned up, and chose a new outfit. Aqua tank, brightly colored floral cargo shorts, and flip-flops with a big flower on top. Not as sexy as the first outfit, but now Erik knew exactly what was underneath.

I ran back downstairs and wiped down the sticky kitchen, made a new pitcher of lemonade, and glanced at the clock. Startled to see it was 4:45 p.m. already, I quickly looked around to make sure everything was ready for guests.

Things seemed perfect until my eyes landed on my dog. I had been so preoccupied with unstickying myself and the kitchen, I'd never given Molly a second thought. She was lying in the doorway to the main floor bedroom, watching me. I cocked my head and she cocked hers in the same direction. Her tail thumped the hardwood floor. I noticed her muzzle seemed wet and bent down to feel it.

"Oh, Molly. Seriously? Lemonade?"

She grinned her answer, licking her chops.

My guests were due in ten minutes and my dog's face was sticky enough to warrant a bath, but that was impossible. I did the best I could with soaking wet paper towels. Molly good-naturedly allowed me the cleansing ritual and tried to help by chewing on the paper towels.

Finally satisfied, I stood up, looked down at myself, and sighed. I was streaked with water, lemonade remnants, and dog hair.

"I give up. I'm simply not meant to look good tonight. And I don't care how much he likes lemonade, I will *never* have it in this house again."

"I'm sorry to hear that," said a male voice from the porch. "And for the record, I think you look gorgeous."

I gasped and laughed at the same time, creating a most *un*gorgeous sound.

"Come in, come in." I laughed. "You never fail to amaze me with your timing."

Erik moved from the porch to the living room, handing me a bouquet of the funkiest flowers I'd ever seen.

"Thank you! I've never seen anything so cool and quirky!" I exclaimed, a huge smile spreading across my face.

Erik's eyes warmed. "Cool and quirky just like you."

Dear God, I prayed silently. *Please don't let me make a total jackass out of myself tonight.* And as an afterthought I added, *And a good night kiss later would be much appreciated.* I didn't think that was asking too much.

Glancing behind Erik, and seeing he was alone, I raised my eyebrow and asked "Dani? Tank?"

"On their way" he said. "Tank needed a walk and a little grooming before coming to visit."

Alone. I was alone with what might be the hottest man on the planet and all I could think about was how sticky and hairy I felt.

"Stop," Erik said, drawing closer to me. "Stop worrying about how you look."

His hand came up and with his index finger, he tilted my chin so I was looking directly into his incredible blue eyes.

"You look amazing," he continued. "The beach agrees with you. Your hair is perfect, your outfit is great and…" His voice trailed off as a wolfish look appeared on his face.

Oh crap. He's thinking about my underwear. Or lack thereof. A shiver ran south from my stomach. His smile spread as if he knew exactly what I was feeling.

Dani and Tank chose that moment to appear on the front porch. Dani looked adorable in cutoffs and a baby doll top. I almost choked again when I noticed that Tank was sporting a big blue bow tied onto his collar. Tank stared back at me defiantly, as if daring me to giggle.

Dropping my gaze and swallowing my laugh, I took the fruit salad Dani was carrying and headed for the kitchen.

Two hours later, we were sitting on the patio in the warm

evening sun, stomachs filled, chatting quietly and laughing while we told dog stories.

Molly and Tank were sacked out at our feet, each having had their own hamburger.

Dani stood, stretching and yawning. "Would you guys mind if I head home? *Runway Divas* premieres at eight and I really want to see it." Dani gave her dad an earnest look, as if sending him a silent message.

"Sure, I don't mind… Sara? Do you?" he said.

Mind? Me? Trying not to sound as eager as I felt and wondering if this was a setup between Dani and her dad, I shooed her home.

"Shall I take Tank with me?" Dani asked.

Hearing his name, Tank opened one eye and glared at Dani. Closing it again, he rolled over, so his back was to us.

Erik laughed. "I guess he wants to stay."

I swear I saw Molly smile.

I brewed coffee and Erik and I made small talk for a while, discussing everything from his writing career and all the places he'd traveled, to the pros and cons of tooth-colored fillings. Before I knew it, darkness was upon us and I stood and started lighting candles. The evening was still warm, and the stars looked amazingly twinkly, or was I just on romantic overload?

"More coffee?" I asked him.

"Sure," he answered. "Love coffee."

"Me too," I said. "I could drink it all day, and some days I do."

"Let me help." Standing, he followed me inside.

Have I mentioned yet how scrumptious he looked in a dark green T-shirt and khaki cargo shorts? The shirt clung to his muscles and the shorts hung on his butt in a way that made me squirm.

Coffees in hand, we headed back to the patio and both sat on the wicker love seat. Turning toward me, Erik's face became serious and in a quiet voice, he thanked me for dinner.

"It was fun. I haven't had an evening like this in a long time," he said.

Oh baby, you ain't seen nothin' yet.

His eyes widened a bit and once again I wondered if he did have the ability to read my mind, or if, God forbid, those words weren't only said to me.

"Sara, do you think we could go out for dinner or a movie sometime?" he asked shyly.

My turn for widened eyes. "I'd love to," I responded, happy I didn't sound too eager, hoping that my "I'd love to" didn't really sound like *Holy crap, are you really asking me out?*

Erik smiled and slid closer to me.

This is it. Finally.

I closed my eyes and leaned toward him. And once again, for the second night in a row, found myself doing a fish imitation instead of a kiss.

I opened my eyes and saw Erik reaching for his cell—it must have been on vibrate. He glanced at the caller ID, tensed, and said softly, "I have to take this. Excuse me for two minutes."

He stood and answered his phone. His back was to me, but the night was quiet, so it wasn't hard to overhear. I started to stand to give him privacy, but he turned and waved me back down.

"John. Hey buddy, how are you? Everything okay?"

I couldn't hear the response, but Erik's shoulders relaxed, so I knew whatever he was hearing wasn't as bad as he had anticipated.

"Excellent. Proud of you, man. You did the right thing."

Erik ended the call and put the cell phone back in his cargo shorts. He sat back down and said, "Sorry about that."

"Hazards of the trade?" I asked, wondering if it had to do with his book.

"No, that was a sponsee of mine." He smiled and said, "Hi. My name is Erik and I'm an alcoholic."

I smiled back at him and said, "Hi, Erik."

He laughed and said, "Did you get that from a TV show?"

"No," I replied. "My brother is in the program. I've been to a few meetings with him to see what it was all about."

"That's excellent. How long has he been sober?"

"Five years," I answered. "I'm so proud of him for changing his life so completely. I thought he was going to die before he found his way to AA."

"Yeah, funny how that happens. Glad he's doing okay. I only work with this one guy. I'm traveling so much that it makes it difficult to sponsor anyone. But I'll be here for an extended period of time, so I wanted to give back while I'm here."

We relaxed back into the love seat, a little closer this time. I wasn't sure if I did that on purpose, or if it was a happy accident that our thighs were lightly touching, that the hair on his legs—a perfect amount of hair I must say—tickled my smooth tan ones…

A warm breeze swirled around us, and a bright moon rose over the ocean.

Erik's hand reached out and tucked an errant piece of hair behind my ear. "Where were we?" he said softly.

I swallowed. I'm not sure why I bothered because there wasn't a drop of spit in my mouth. "I think we were right about… here," I replied, taking matters into my own hands and kissing him lightly on the lips. They were soft and smooth, and I was ever so tempted to run my tongue against them but figured that might be taking things too fast.

Imagine my surprise when I felt Erik's tongue running along *my* lips. *Great minds think alike* was my first thought. My second, coming right on the heels of the first, was *Holy crap.*

Our first kiss deepened, and Erik's hands came up to hold my face.. I didn't quite know what to do with my hands, so I kept them in my lap and enjoyed having my mouth claimed by the hottest man I'd ever kissed.

Erik pulled his lips off mine but kept his hands on my face, gently holding me. A slow smile spread across his face as he gazed into my eyes. "That was nice, Sara."

"Yes," I whispered, not trusting my voice yet. At least the saliva problem had rectified itself. Now I was more concerned I would drool.

"May I kiss you again?" he asked.

Seriously? He had to ask?

"Yes, please."

"I like that… yes, please." Erik chuckled and once again his lips met mine.

We sat on the love seat, under the full moon, the ocean breeze moving over us, and we made out like two high school kids. Just when I thought my body would explode like Fourth of July fireworks, he broke our kiss and sat back. "I get a little performance anxiety when I'm being stared at." He laughed.

I looked down and saw Molly and Tank at our feet, both sitting there with smiles, tongues out and tails wagging. Well, Molly was smiling and wagging. Tank was more of a jowly grimace and a hiney shake.

I didn't know whether to laugh or cry. "Timing is everything in life," I said, sighing.

"In your case that is truer than with most people, don't you think?" Erik asked.

Laughing, I smacked his arm. "Are you complaining?"

"Oh, hell no!" he said. "I've enjoyed every single voyeuristic moment."

My cheeks burned and he laughed. "Sara... you're blushing."

I dropped my eyes to my Hot Pinky Toe-painted toes. "I'm just thinking about how many embarrassing things you've caught me doing. I'm surprised you aren't running in the opposite direction."

Erik rolled his eyes. "Are you kidding? I keep getting teased, one body part at a time. I figure by the end of the summer, I will be able to put all the puzzle pieces together."

End of the summer? How cute that he thinks I'll make him wait that long. I squirmed in anticipation.

Reaching out, he ran his finger down my jawline. "Thank you for dinner and dessert." When he said *dessert* he raised an eyebrow. "I think it's a good time for me to take myself home."

I stared at my toes and contemplated whether asking him to stay would be a good idea or not. If he said no, it would crush my ego to no end, successfully wiping out any good memories of the evening. If he said yes, he *might* think me too easy and that *might* impact any future we *might* have. So, I decided it was a bad idea, looked into his gorgeous eyes, and smiled. "Thank you for an amazing evening."

We stood, and he grabbed both my hands. "Thank you. We'll do that dinner soon, okay?" And before I could answer, he leaned in and gave me a soft, quick kiss.

We exchanged cell phone numbers with the promise of that dinner on the horizon.

Before I retired for the night, I powered up the laptop and filled the Cell in on all the happenings. "I could really fall for this guy," I typed. "He's amazing in every sense of the word."

I fielded a few questions about Erik's kissing technique: Wet? Dry? Too much tongue? I answered as best I could until they were finally satisfied, and I took myself and my furry friend and went to sleep.

CHAPTER 5

The next morning dawned cool and rainy. Molly was in no hurry to leave her half of the bed, so we snuggled a little. Spooning with a large golden retriever was almost as satisfying as being spooned by a hot guy.

I said *almost*.

As my fingers toyed with Molly's soft ears, I let my mind wander, and of course it wandered next door. Could I see this going somewhere? Could I see a future for myself with Erik? Could I imagine myself a stepmother to Dani? Could I *be* any more of an idiot? Erik was a famous writer. His books sold millions. He was gorgeous, charming, and probably had a girl in every city. No doubt, he broke hearts on a monthly basis, and if I didn't rein in my heart, it would be next in line.

Commotion outside the house got me out of bed and in front of my window. Molly chuffed, and I wasn't sure if it was because of the noise outside, or the fact that her ear massage had ended abruptly.

I looked to my left toward Erik's place and not a soul was stirring in the gray drizzle. The only things moving out front were the waves and two surfers. My eyes moved along to the right, to the gorgeous home on the other side of me. It had been vacant since I moved in, but apparently it wasn't going to remain that way.

The commotion came from a very squeaky luggage cart being rolled up the boardwalk and through the front door of the house. I squinted, trying to get a better look at the person pulling the cart. My mind ticked off each item as it registered in my now wide-awake brain.

Female. Forties. Built. Red hair. Tall. Damn it.

Pulling up the rear of the cart, carrying a backpack and grocery bags, was a young girl who looked around Dani's age. No guy in sight.

Double damn it.

I watched as the fantasy of a future with Erik flew out of my head, landed on the sidewalk below, ran to the ocean, and dove into the waves, never to return. "Stupid fantasy anyway," I mumbled. Molly raised an eyebrow at me. Or at least raised the location above her eye that would have held an eyebrow.

"What?" I asked her. "You don't think she'll be all over him in a New York minute? You don't think Dani and that girl will become best buddies?"

I swear my dog rolled her eyes at me.

"Fine." I stomped my way into the bathroom.

When I emerged, all fresh and invigorated, Molly was waiting for me, leash in mouth. I quickly dressed in gray yoga pants, a tight white tank top, and flip-flops. I tousled my wet hair into messy waves, put on mascara, and went downstairs.

Molly cocked her head at me. "What now? My outfit?" I looked down at myself. I was fine. I was more than fine. "Oh," I said. "You think I look sexier than normal for a morning walk, don't you?"

Seventy-five pounds of golden fur grinned at me.

I clucked my tongue. "Nonsense."

I clipped on the leash and the two of us headed outside. The drizzle had stopped, but the morning remained gray, the sky dark with threatening rain. I glanced over at the house to my right, hoping to catch a glimpse of the new people, praying to see a male figure there with them.

As luck would have it, I saw the two females. And as *my* luck would have it, no male. The woman glanced my way and I raised my hand in a wave.

A smile appeared on her lips, but it never reached her eyes, which were a frosty shade of green. She had a weird energy about her, almost jagged and sharp.

"Hi there," I said. "Sara Maloney. This is Molly." I pointed to the furball standing next to me.

"Nice to meet you, Sara," the woman said, her eyes moving over me in silent appraisal. "Andrea Harris. People call me Drea."

Drea was certainly attractive enough. A little taller than me. *Of course, who isn't?* Curvier than me. I also noticed she was quite chilly. Don't ask.

Her red hair was cut in a stylish short bob and her skin had obviously never had a zit or a wrinkle. I hated her already.

Covering my hatred with a fake smile of my own, I said, "Welcome to the neighborhood. How long are you staying?"

Tapping a finely manicured fingernail against her too-white

laminated front teeth, she said, "Through mid-July, so about a month."

I think I was still smiling but wasn't quite sure. Something about Drea was rubbing me the wrong way.

"Is that your daughter?" I asked, nodding at the teenager who had suddenly appeared behind Drea.

Drea glanced over her shoulder. "Carolyn! I didn't hear you come out. Meet our neighbor, um… Sally was it?"

"Sara. Hi, Carolyn, nice to meet you."

Carolyn mumbled something. I think it was "Hello," but it could have been "meatball." Drea rolled her perfectly done smoky eyes. "Teenagers. Can't live with 'em, can't kill 'em."

Never having had a teenager of my own, I didn't know if that was a normal reaction, or if Drea could possibly be a homicidal maniac in the making. We exchanged a few more pleasantries and I learned that Drea was newly divorced <sigh> from a much older man (*her* words). And she was apparently planning to have a month-long *Look at me! I'm single, hot, and rich* beach party. This last part, of course, was all concocted in my brain.

Molly gave my leg a gentle bump with her nose, reminding me that we were outside for a reason. As I started to say my good-byes, I heard Erik's screen door open and close, the sound of Tank's paws moving across the deck, and his low woof when he saw Molly. I closed my eyes briefly and said a small prayer that Dani was the human that stepped out behind Tank.

"Tank, hush," Erik said in his early morning sexy voice.

Damn it. The universe has a wicked sense of humor.

I snuck a quick look behind me. Erik was standing on his front patio in a pair of well-fitting, faded jeans and a white T-shirt. Also well fitting. Bare feet. Hair wet and tousled. Coffee mug in his hand. Perfection walking.

He saw the three of us standing there, and ambled over. Tank followed, making a beeline for Molly. Erik came up beside me, ruffled Molly's ears, slung his free arm around my neck, and kissed my cheek.

My brain tried to register what was happening. Unfortunately, the part of the brain that is used for logic was completely MIA. Erik removed his hand from my neck and put it out to shake Drea's.

"Good morning, I'm Erik Hanson. I live next door to Sara."

Drea slowly put out her hand to shake Erik's. I watched her eyes take in the male specimen in front of her. Her pupils dilated and her breath grew a bit labored. Her smile reached her eyes this time and she flashed her pearly whites. *She'd better not flash her 34DDs or there'll be some ass kicking in the sand.*

As if on cue, she managed to appear chilly again.

"Hello, Erik" she purred. Seriously. She purred like a cat. "Drea Harris. This is my daughter, Carolyn."

Carolyn was staring at Erik with a mixture of anger and apathy. That's a hard mixture to attain, but Carolyn did it well. Erik shook her hand and once again, Carolyn's response could have been "Hi" or "meatball."

Drea kneeled and clucked her tongue at Tank. "Who do we have here?"

"That's Tank, but don't get any ideas. He's totally smitten with Molly," Erik said laughingly.

Drea glanced sharply at Erik. The look in her eyes told me

she might have the looks and body, but she lacked a sense of humor.

Tank looked at Drea suspiciously. He ambled over to within a foot of her and sat down in the sand. A low growl came from his throat.

"Tank," Erik said firmly. "*No* growling." Tank glanced at Erik as if to say, *I don't like her, and I want her to know it, and I think somebody said meatball.*

It was at that moment I knew I would love Tank for the rest of my life. Molly bumped me again. I didn't really want to leave Erik and Drea alone, but Molly was getting antsy. As much as I wished she would simply empty her bladder on Drea's Manolo Blahnik's—completely inappropriate for the beach, by the way—I knew that was wrong and took my leave from the group.

"I'm sure I will see you later," I said to Drea and Carolyn. "Come on, girl."

Glancing back, I saw Drea, who was still crouched down near Tank, put her hand out to Erik for some help standing up.

Erik looked at me with a bemused smile and waved at me before extending his hand to Drea.

Molly and I took our time and when we returned, there was no one in sight. My imagination was trying to get me to believe that Erik was inside Drea's house at that moment, helping her move in, and perhaps eyeballing those chilly DDs. I shook off the image and went inside. Since it wasn't a beach day and my house was clean and stocked from the day before, I devoted myself to creating.

I quickly sketched out a girl's face on some vellum, sealed it, and adhered it to a canvas panel. I added watercolor crayons and pencils and some white gesso and brought the girl to life with color. Layer after layer brought new dimension to her. I watched as she morphed from a pencil sketch to a face. Once I was satisfied with her tones and shadows, I sealed her once again and started her hair. Cutting strips of old book paper, I sealed them down and added dragonflies to the strands.

Before I knew it, it was lunchtime. I padded barefoot to the kitchen and glanced in the refrigerator. Nothing appealed. All I wanted was to get back to my canvas. So I took a paper cup, filled it halfway with honey-roasted peanuts, grabbed a bottle of water, and went back to my makeshift studio.

Molly followed me, knowing full well that a cup of nuts, tipped at *just* the right angle to my mouth was sure to result in a nut or two falling to the floor.

After our snack and a quick walk in the drizzle, I returned to my project. Molly curled up by the front door with a watchful eye outside. There wasn't much for her to watch—the fog and grayness of the day made for a very desolate beach and boards. At one point in the afternoon, Dani came out holding Tank on a leash with one hand and typing quickly on her cell phone with the other. They weren't outside long when I heard a distinctive clicking on the boards in front of my house.

Drea teetered toward Dani and Tank, trying to negotiate her way without catching one of her heels in the space between the boards. I knew my ticket to hell was paid in full when I found myself hoping she'd fall flat on her pretty face. Although she'd probably fall on her boobs and bounce right back up again.

Dani was also watching Drea approach, her thumbs pausing mid-text as Drea turned to walk onto Dani's patio. I sensed more than heard Tank's growl, mostly because I could see Drea pause, her fake smile frozen in place. I cursed the humidity that had forced me to close the windows and turn on the air conditioning that morning. I couldn't hear a thing.

Smiling at the woman, Dani leaned over to pat Tank's head in a soothing way. I watched and wished I could read lips as Drea and Dani exchanged a few words, Drea keeping a safe distance from Tank the Fierce. Her eyes kept shifting from Dani to the house, and I knew she was watching for Erik. At that moment, my cell ding-donged, meaning a new text message had arrived.

ERIK

THAT woman is outside my house.

SARA

I know. I'm watching her closely.

ERIK

She scares me a bit.

SARA

Me too.

ERIK

I think she's got designs on me.

SARA

Because she's stalking your house?

ERIK

No. Because after you walked away earlier, she asked me to come over for drinks.

My stomach dropped a bit.

SARA

Did you say yes?

ERIK

Are you serious?

SARA

So, did you say yes?

ERIK

Sara. Stop it. I told her I was already involved.

My stomach dropped a little more as I hoped—but wasn't positive—he meant me.

SARA

With?

ERIK

Seriously?

SARA

Well, I hate assuming things.

ERIK

You make me laugh.

With a smile, I put the phone down and went back to my sentry duties. Drea had given up on Erik coming out and was teetering back to her own house. I waved at her from the porch, trying not to let my face turn smug. Smugness would only serve to make me look like an idiot if things didn't work out the way I hoped they would.

Drea waved back at me in a dejected manner, and the smile that never quite reached her eyes wasn't as bright as before. I almost felt sorry for her. *Almost* being the operative word.

Dani was still out front with Tank, her gaze following Drea's retreating back. After Drea entered her house, Dani and Tank walked over and joined me on the porch.

"What do you think of her?" Dani asked.

Not wanting to pass judgment on anyone, I kept it neutral. "I think that she is very pretty and is probably lonely."

Dani raised an eyebrow at me. "No. Tell me what you think of her."

Damn kid was too savvy for me.

Trying again, I said, "Well, she's definitely not a happy person. And I think she has an interest in getting to know your father better." A little butterfly flitted across my belly when I said the words aloud.

Dani grinned. "That's better," she said. "I get a weird vibe off her. She asked me if I wanted to come over later and hang out with her daughter."

"Are you going to? She might be a nice girl…" My voice trailed off as I tried to picture Dani and Carolyn conversing.

"It's called Hot Pinky Toe, do you like it?"
"Meatball."

Dani scuffed her toe on the floor and chewed her lower lip. "Not sure. I'd like to meet people, but I'm just not sure."

I told her to follow her heart and conscience. "There's no harm in trying. You guys might become fast friends, like you and me."

Dani nodded. "Maybe I'll walk over there and see if she wants to take a walk with me and Tank."

I watched as she went next door and knocked. Carolyn opened the door and I could see the two of them exchange introductions. And then I watched as Dani walked back to my house, alone.

"No interest?" I asked her.

"She said she was busy and maybe another time," Dani responded. "That or she said something about meatballs for dinner."

Chuckling, I handed Dani a blank canvas and said, "Have at it."

We happily painted and collaged for a couple of hours, the gray day a welcome respite from the early summer sun and activities.

That night, long after Dani went back home, I sat on the porch in the dark and listened to Erik spinning tunes again. The man had great taste in music. A mix of blues, country, singer-songwriter, and some golden oldies were in his mix tonight.

My phone ding-donged a text arrival.

ERIK

Is the music too loud?

SARA

Not at all. Enjoying it.

ERIK

Why don't you come over and hear it with me?

I almost forgot to type my affirmative response in my mad dash to repair hair, makeup, and clothing.

The humidity had cleared out and I was able to leave my hair long and wavy. Since it was still a little cool, I chose jeans and a long-sleeved T-shirt, flip-flops and lip gloss. I instructed Molly to hold down the fort and walked over to Erik's home.

Tank greeted me when I knocked on the door, his butt wagging and his eyes looking beyond me to see if Molly was there.

"Sorry, buddy, no Molly tonight." I swear that dog looked sad.

Erik leaned over Tank to open the screen door to let me in. As I walked past him, I handed him an icy cold bottle of sparkling mineral water and two plastic wineglasses. He smiled and leaned down to brush a quick kiss on my lips before moving toward the kitchen to pour us a drink.

While he was busy doing that, I looked around his home. It was an open floor plan, the front door leading into a huge living area and kitchen, with stairs leading to the second floor in the back of the house. Another door led to what I assumed was the bathroom. From the sound of water running from behind it, I was certain I was right. Dani emerged from behind that closed door and squealed with delight when she saw me standing there.

"Yay! You came over! That's so awesome. I knew my dad was going to ask. I'm totally going to leave you guys alone. I just downloaded the whole season of *Hot Blooded*, so you won't even know I'm here." She finally took a breath and stopped talking.

"We're just going to listen to some music and talk. You don't have to disappear," I said.

Of course, my brain was saying, *Disappear. Disappear. Disappear.* Feeling guilty, yet not, relief filled me when Dani trotted up the stairs and disappeared into her room. As much as I loved her company, time alone with Erik was front and center in my mind.

I sat down on one of the comfy-looking couches and kicked off my flip-flops. Tucking one foot under me, I looked around at the room. For only having been here a month, Erik had decorated the place with style and beauty. Shelf after shelf of bestsellers lined one wall, and a quick glance told me none of his books were on there. *Humble and hot at the same time.*

Tank strolled over and sat on my foot. He leaned against me and breathed heavily in his raspy, gurgly way.

"I like you too, my friend." I scratched him behind the ears.

"He's smitten with you," Erik said. "Although I think he prefers Molly, you are the next best thing since you smell like her."

I guess my eyes must have registered horror at the thought of smelling like a golden retriever, because Erik quickly tried to explain what he meant. "Not that you smell like a dog. I didn't mean it that way, honest. You smell fabulous, like sexy incense or something, not like Molly at all. I only meant Tank can smell Molly on you because dogs can smell things that humans can't."

Stopping, he took a deep breath and stood there with his cheeks all puffed out waiting for my response.

I could see where Dani got her ability to spew long sentences without taking a breath.

"For a man who makes his living with words, you're lacking a bit in choice." I grinned and batted my lashes at him. Lash batting doesn't come as second nature to me, and immediately my left eye started to twitch.

Erik chuckled softly and handed me my glass. We clinked plastic and silently toasted each other with smiles and sighs. I think we both knew where this was heading. Maybe not tonight, but soon, this man would be mine.

The rest of the evening passed in a smooth, easy, and relaxed way. I was amazed at how comfortable I felt in Erik's presence, like I could be myself without worrying about how dorky, geeky, or clumsy I was. After all, he'd witnessed some of my most memorable humiliations and still stuck around to get to know me better. That, or he liked the body part teases.

At midnight, after finishing two bottles of the sparkling water, multiple CDs, and fifteen different conversation topics, I stood up to leave. Holding out my hands, I pulled Erik up from the comfy couch. As he rose, he slipped his hands out of mine and around my waist. This time I knew exactly what to do with my hands. I ran them through his gorgeous curls and grasped the back of his neck, pulling his lips to mine. His tongue parted my lips and ran across my teeth, causing chills to stream from my lower back all the way to the top of my head.

The kiss deepened as he held me tighter and his hands lightly rubbed my back, covering the exact path that the chills had taken seconds before. We leaned back in our embrace and looked at each other with slow, lazy, happy smiles.

Until Mother Nature reared her ugly head, that is. Unfortunately for us both, there are two downsides to sparkling water. One, it causes me to burp. Two, liquid goes in, liquid must come out, and it was at this moment my bladder chose to let me know it was time.

I stifled a burp and giggled, which made me burp again. Erik laughed that low, sexy laugh that made me squirm in my seat even when I wasn't sitting. My bladder ramped up its insistence, so I excused myself and went to the bathroom. After taking care of business, I looked in the mirror and gazed at the woman looking back. Hair a bit disheveled, lips puffy and soft, eyes sleepy with a smudge of mascara underneath.

"You're falling in love, Sara," I whispered. "Are you ready for this?"

Hell yes!!! my inner badass goddess screamed.

I exited the bathroom after fixing that smudge and swearing up and down that I'd invest in waterproof mascara the next day to prevent smudging. Hard to remove though. I'd tried everything and sometimes it never fully came off until it just plain wore off.

I found Erik in the kitchen studying the contents of the pantry like he was perusing a menu.

"What are you looking for?" I asked.

Startled, he spun around with a sheepish grin. "I didn't hear you come out of the bathroom," he said. "Truthfully? I have no clue what I'm looking for in here. I had this crazy thought about trying to entice you to stay longer if I had cookies or something."

Like he needs cookies. I stepped forward into his arms and stared into his eyes, wondering what the hell just happened to the rest of my life.

Erik tipped his head slightly and planted a kiss on my forehead. Amazing how a forehead kiss can weaken one's knees when one is quickly, yet smoothly, falling in love.

"You know I want you to stay, right?" he murmured.

I nodded, feeling a little flutter of butterflies in my stomach.

"But it probably wouldn't be a great idea. Dani…" He paused, his eyes shifting toward the staircase. "I know she adores you, but I'm not sure how she'd feel about us jumping into bed in the room next to hers."

As the words left his mouth, his eyes registered the shock and dismay at what he'd just said. "Not that we'd end up in bed. I didn't mean that the way it sounded." Beads of sweat popped up ever so slightly at his sexy hairline.

I could have let him off the hook. I could have. But this was much too much fun. I widened my eyes, feigning outrage. As my eyes widened, his eyes did the same, and the thought of the two of us standing there in the kitchen, at 12:43 a.m., wrapped in each other's arms, all puffed up with fake outrage and outright terror? That thought made me chortle. Loudly.

His arms tightened around me as my attempt at humor became apparent to him. The chortling was the big clue I guess. "Cute, aren't you? You were going to let me suffer, weren't you?"

I got up on my tiptoes and kissed him on the end of his nose. "I got ya, champ. I knew what you meant… or didn't mean." I smiled, and he smiled, and we walked back to the living room hand in hand.

"I like you, Sara." And then he did it. He did the Harry Christmas voice from *Dumb and Dumber.* "I like you a LOT." Then grinned his sexy, wolfish grin.

It was in that moment that I knew. I knew beyond a shadow of a doubt I was in love. My inner doubting voice didn't have a chance. The badass goddess took her out at the knees before the thought of *Too soon, too soon* could enter my brain. Another thing I knew in that split second between "I like you a LOT" and my lips hitting his was this… he was feeling much the same as I was.

It was going to be a good summer, Tater.

CHAPTER 6

You're probably thinking I stayed, aren't you? Or you're guessing I invited Erik back to my place where we wouldn't have to worry about Dani hearing or seeing something we'd regret. Now that I think of it, that would have been a stellar idea. But no, after that kiss, I said good night and reluctantly we parted ways. As I opened the porch door to the Pendleton, my phone dinged a text message arriving. I chuckled when I saw who it was from.

ERIK

I miss you already.

Do you ever have one of those surreal moments where you're not quite sure if you're actually in your life or someone else's and you're watching it in a movie? That's what this felt like. Now came the angst over how to answer. This could take a while.

It was almost like when I needed to choose a font for a

project. I could get lost for hours on a font site. Same with emoticons. But I didn't have hours. I chewed on my lower lip for a moment—still a little puffy from all the making out—and felt out each possible response.

I could say, "I miss you too, babe" and leave it at that or I could leave off the *babe*, or I could follow it up with "See you tomorrow…" as a strong confident woman, or should it be "See you tomorrow?" like I shouldn't just expect it? *This is what I do to myself. I worry about the littlest of things at the oddest of times.*

> I miss you too…

I gulped and continued

> see you tomorrow…

and added a winky face. A winky face makes everything more lighthearted. In most situations, you can't go wrong with the winky face.

And then I waited, still standing on the porch where I was when I first received his text. I waited, and I waited a moment longer and that's when I realized I hadn't budged from my spot in a good five minutes. I hadn't even woken up Molly, who I'm sure was already upstairs in bed, and that's when another realization came to me. Slowly I looked to my right… out the window toward Erik's front door where I spotted him, leaning against his doorjamb with his phone in his hand, watching me, perfectly lit in the moonlight, standing there waiting for a return text.

At least in the moonlight he couldn't really see the blush that started somewhere around my ankles and whooshed up to the top of my head. He couldn't see my eyes, which were darting from one direction to another even though I hadn't turned my head back to my front door. I watched him slowly raise the phone and start typing. He made a little production out of hitting Send and then leaned back against the doorway and smiled.

When my phone dinged I glanced down, clenching my teeth like the awkward, not confident woman I really was.

> Sara, I'm hoping you're going to see me in all your tomorrows…

I looked up from the phone and into Erik's face, which was partially shadowed. We stared like that for a moment, each of us lost in thought. He straightened up and walked across the moonlit sand to my porch door. I opened it, my heart beating so hard I could barely breathe.

Thank God I was able to get one breath in before he grabbed me and kissed me.

Kissed me hard.

Tongue.

Hands.

Grasping hair.

Gasps.

Hands.

Wandering.

Playing.

Arousing.

Heat.

Tongues.

Breathless promises.

Hands…

Breathe, Sara, breathe.

I realized we were still standing on the porch around the same time Molly realized I was home and there was "company." She wandered onto the porch with us, making things rather crowded. And then before I could say or do anything, she nosed Erik right in the crotch to say hello.

The look on Erik's face made me wonder if we'd be able to continue our dalliance this evening. Assuming we were going to have a dalliance, which I'm pretty sure we were. Or as close to a dalliance as you could get without actually completing the act.

Erik recovered quickly after a whoosh of air escaped his mouth and another whoosh went right back in. Molly wagged her tail in apology and he ruffled her fur, and all was well in Sara's world.

"I need to let her out for a quick tinkle. Make yourself at home."

"Wait a minute," Erik said. "I have a better idea. I'll walk Molly. You go make yourself comfortable, and I'll go walk off this almost devastating groin versus dog head thing."

Smart man. He knows women.

"Oh," he added, "but it's up to you to find the perfect music for us. 'Cuz you know every time either of us hears anything that's played tonight it will bring us back to this moment. This magical evening. This poetic perfection of time."

"Okay, now you're just screwing with me," I interrupted his dialogue before I started laughing. "Poetic perfection of time?

C'mon. You're a freaking writer, what the hell is 'poetic perfection of time' supposed to mean?"

"And now you're just screwing with me and not in the way I intend for the remainder of this night," he shot back at me with a huge grin.

I threw him Molly's leash and headed inside to 'get comfortable.' *I'll show him poetic perfection of time.*

I ran upstairs and drew a quick shower, thanking the universe for the aforethought to shave my legs that morning. Literally five minutes later, I was showered and lotioned, my hair retousled and face washed, so I didn't have to worry about it later. But now the drama of what to put on was upon me.

Big furry robe with nothing underneath.

Sexy robe with nothing underneath.

Both options above with a thong and sexy bra.

Barefoot? Slippers? Flip-flops?

I chewed my dang lip again. Another mental note to stop doing that. It's bad for you. I went with sexy robe, sexy matching bra underneath. No undies. After all, he'd already seen the bra-thong combo through my back door. He only had one last surprise left. Why make it any more difficult for him to access? Poor man had worked hard enough today, what with all that kissing and crap. A swipe of clear gloss so that I wouldn't chew on my lower lip and I called myself good. The hard part came next: picking out the music.

Since he had a definite bent toward singer-songwriter with some R & B-soul-jazz on the side, I filled my phone's playlist with a plethora of names like James Hunter, Jason Isbell, Brandi Carlile, and the like. Everything I chose was sexy, a lot of rhythm and all the things that made me wiggle in my seat.

I tidied up the living room and started the music, which played through the entire house by way of strategically placed speakers and the magic of Bluetooth. Modern technology. Thirty-five years ago I would have been in here frantically trying to create a mix tape. I lit a stick of Om Nag Champa incense, put a chewy bone out for Molly to keep her busy and out of Erik's crotch, and started a pot of coffee.

Holy crap, I'm going to have sex. The thought popped into my head with no warning. Followed quickly by *Holy crap, I'm going to have sex* again because it had been a while, damn it. I let that thought settle in for a moment and tested myself for how I felt about it.

What a waste of three seconds that was. Bring on the man.

As perfect timing would have it—*who says you can't manifest your perfect life?*—Erik was walking up the front path with Molly.

I stood in the doorway between the living room and porch, backlit. Sexy robe. Barefoot. I knew the picture I made in front of him and arched my back a bit to make it even sexier. Except that when you arch, make sure you know where the air ends and the doorjamb begins so as not to slam your head against said doorjamb. Tears came to my eyes and at that moment, I was very glad I had washed my face and mascara off or I would have been a streaky mess. I glanced at the porch door, which by now Erik had opened, and before I could wonder how much he saw, he asked me if my head hurt.

Laughing I said, "No, and get used to that. I do things like bump heads and fall down a lot, you know."

That got me an eye roll and a head shake. "No shit," he

deadpanned. "Shall I recite the list of what I've already witnessed to date?"

That got him what I'd hoped looked like a smirk, but I think the blush just made it look like a grimacing hot flash.

Erik bent down to unhook Molly's leash and got rewarded with a big wet kiss. From Molly, not me. Not yet anyway. He ruffled her head as a thank-you and was rewarded with a squinty-eyed grin. From Molly, not me. "She adores you," I said with my own squinty-eyed smile.

Erik straightened up and reached for my hand. "I adore her right back. Now let me take a good look at you because I'm pretty sure you're taking my breath away." He put his hands on my shoulders and his gaze went from the top of my still hurting head slowly down to the tips of my bare toes. His face grew serious and his breath caught in his throat. "Sara... do you have any idea how beautiful you are?"

It had been a long time since anyone told me I was beautiful. Or pretty. Or cute. Or not so bad for an old bag. I dropped my head and shook it side to side. Erik took his hand from my shoulder and tipped my chin up so my eyes met his. His eyes were tender.

Holy crap this man is incredible.

"Sara, you are beautiful," he stated in a low, sexy voice. "I'm sorry you haven't been told that every day of your life. I'm going to make sure that changes."

And then he kissed me. Every nerve ending in my body lit up like Clark Griswold's house in *National Lampoon's Christmas Vacation*. My toes curled as the kiss deepened and Erik's warm hands rubbed circles on my back. As he pulled his mouth from mine I could sense his smile. I could *hear* his smile. I opened my eyes and sure enough, he was grinning from ear to ear.

"Sara, come with me for a minute." He pulled me out the porch door onto the front walk. "Look how incredible the sky is tonight," he said, pointing upward.

We stood there several moments gazing at the moon and stars. Erik stood behind me, his arms wrapped around my body. He tipped his head down until his lips met my ear. His warm breath tickled my neck and made my body hum of its own accord. I'm not exaggerating; my body had a mind of its own. Forgetting we were standing a few feet off the boardwalk and in full view of anyone and everyone, my butt decided to lightly rub itself against this man who held me tightly against him. If I wasn't so against sand in uncomfortable places I would have taken him right there in my front yard. I suspect Erik felt the same. Actually, I had hard evidence that he did actually feel the same.

As I was debating the whole sand in bad places thing in my head, Erik chuckled softly and whispered, "Look who's watching us."

Following his gaze without being conspicuous, I saw Drea looking down at us from a lit second-floor window. We were standing in the bright moonlight, so I knew she could see us quite clearly. I'm not sure Drea realized how clearly we could see her.

Every so often I'd have to tamp down the badass goddess that wanted me to do reckless crap. Right at that moment, she wanted me to risk the sand. Just to show Drea she was shit out of luck. But that little bit of recklessness could get us in way too much trouble. So logic ruled, and I simply raised my arm and gave her a slight wave. I could see her startle as she realized we could see her, and she awkwardly waved back and moved away from the window.

I grabbed Erik's hand and said, "Let's get inside and away from prying eyes."

At this point, we both realized how late it was, almost 1:00 a.m. Erik grasped my hand and with a questioning look put the decision in my hands whether to proceed with the night or realize we were not spring chickens and should retire to our respective beds. So I did what any self-respecting, mature, independent woman would do. I made coffee. Lots of strong, black coffee.

Erik was stretched out in the recliner, his mug of steaming energy resting in his lap. I curled up on the sofa and tucked my legs and feet under me. My robe fell away from my chest, showing the lacy bra underneath. Before I could blink, Erik was next to me on the couch, teasing the already pulled-away robe even further with his index finger. His lips fell to my neck, eliciting sighs from me and an impromptu butt wiggle. After he was done nuzzling my neck, his finger nudged the robe off my left shoulder and his lips followed his finger. Lightly planting kisses all over my shoulder and upper arm, he edged my bra strap off my shoulder, and his lips made their way to the curve of my breast not covered by lace. I knew at that moment I was putty in his hands.

His lips broke away from my skin and he looked at me and in a husky voice said, "Baby... I hope you want me as much as

I want you at this moment." And he almost looked concerned. Then the wolf grin appeared again as he pointed to my still moving hips. "Having an issue down there?"

Laughing, I lightly grabbed his head, kissed him, and said, "Yes. And it desperately needs attention." I decided to do a sexy striptease to the song that started playing. An earthy bump-and-grind kind of striptease. Erik settled back on the couch, a bemused look on his face. I was doing a sexy little barefoot shuffle as I attempted to untie my satin robe, which refused to cooperate. I started to sweat a little from fighting the frustrating knot.

I can hear you all now. *"Why did you knot it, Sara? Why not an easy open bow?"* In my defense, have you ever tried to keep a satin robe on and tied *without* a double knot? It would slide right open. *I rest my case.*

But back to the sweating. Erik sensed my frustration and pulled me toward him to help me. Within about thirty seconds, he was also sweating and had almost cracked a tooth trying to budge the tight satin with his front teeth. He sat back a moment, then stood and walked stiffly to my porch-studio area. I heard some rustling and then he returned with my scissors. Which he used to cut the band of satin that kept him from his bounty.

As my robe fell open to his hungry eyes, the final "piece" of the body puzzle came into play. In a low, serious voice he said, "Let's go to the bedroom."

Erik pulled me into his arms and kissed me softly. "Let's both get a few hours of sleep. I'll see you after that."

He started to walk away but turned back and said, "We're going to have to tell Dani that our relationship has moved to a new level."

"I know. Together or separate?" I asked.

"I want to say together," he said, "but that's just me being a big chicken and not knowing what to do with a sixteen-year-old daughter who thinks everything you do deserves an eye roll."

With that, Erik patted my sex knot, turned, and as silently as possible entered his house, giving me a wave and blowing me a kiss before closing the door. I walked back to my porch door and I heard a *Pssssst* coming from the second floor of Erik's house. Dani was at the window grinning down at me.

"Egads, Dani, you almost gave me heart failure!" I hissed up at her, my heart pounding and my bowels feeling suspiciously watery.

"Sorry. I couldn't help overhearing some of that, and I want you to know I'm really happy, but I'm worried about that knot," she said with a wicked grin.

Letting out a laugh, I looked up at her, the dawn giving me enough light to see her face. "Thank you. That makes me very happy. I'll deal with you later on the hair thing. We'll talk more later today, okay?" I blew her a kiss and went inside. My still warm bed—thank you, Molly—enveloped my body and dragged me into slumber.

CHAPTER 7

When I cracked my eyes open at 8:00 a.m. it was not because I'd had enough sleep. It was not because the sun was shining brightly into my bedroom. It was not because someone was hammering. No, the stealer of my snoozing was the furface snoring loudly beside me. I stretched and yawned, a delicious soreness running through my body. Erik had a master's degree in the art of arousing women. He'd brought me to brinks I'd never thought possible, which kind of explained that knot. I grimaced when I remembered how much extra effort my shower was going to take this morning. Molly had given up on the belly rubs but not the bed. She stretched and jumped off the bed. Her tail wagging, she trotted to the stairs, obviously more chipper than I was feeling.

Oh crap. Is she telling me she needs a walk? I was standing there in my bedroom, in my oversized T-shirt, with a gigantic hair bundle growing out of the back of my head. There was no way I could risk this, could I? Molly's bark from downstairs made up my mind for me. I pulled on a pair of baggy shorts and grabbed a ball cap before clipping on her leash.

Ten minutes later, I was back inside without incident. A dark, cloudy day kept the eyes to a minimum on the boardwalk. I stripped off my shirt and shorts and jumped in the shower, along with the cup of coffee I'd started before walking Molly. The challenge was in not watering down your coffee with shower spray. Or soap bubbles.

First things first, I soaked my head with water and rubbed a handful of conditioner throughout the knot. Slowly but surely it came loose, and I was glad to see that I didn't lose too many hairs in the deconstruction.

After finishing in the bathroom, I pulled on multicolored yoga pants and a simple white tee. It was humid and cloudy and I hoped a thunderstorm wasn't in our future. I checked my face in the magnifying mirror. That probably wasn't my brightest idea. The dark circles threatened to take over my face, so I swiped on some "age rewinding" cover-up under my eyes and a little mascara. I pulled my wet hair back into a low ponytail and took a long look at myself in the mirror.

I looked tired, which made sense since I only got a few hours of sleep. My lips were still puffy, and I had a few muscles throughout my body that were screaming about being woken up after a long slumber. But there was something about my eyes. More than just the bags and dark circles, there was a glow in my face that screamed *I HAD SEX LAST NIGHT* so loudly that I knew it was visible to anyone looking at me. I smiled at my reflection and knew that glow included a healthy dose of love. New love. A tingle went through my body as I thought about the early morning hours and all the early morning hours I knew were in my future.

Though I wanted to skip downstairs, I wasn't a complete idiot, so I skipped down them in my mind while keeping my hand firmly on the handrail as I carefully made my way down. I poured a fresh cup of coffee—because diluted and bubbles—and looked out my kitchen window, sipping the much-needed black magic. I was daydreaming, not realizing Erik was standing at his kitchen window also, directly across from me. There was a mug in his hand and a smile on his face as he watched me become aware of his presence.

Smiling in return, I gave him a little wave. He raised his mug, and his eyebrows, then pointed toward the front yard. I nodded *yes* and padded my way through the house and out the porch door.

When I exited, Erik was coming out his front door at the same time. We met on the sand, right around the spot where I dug the hole for my tatas. His free arm reached for me and enveloped my body in a hug. His lips found mine and his stubbly chin scratched my cheeks and I didn't care a bit. *Oh my gawd I can't get enough of this man.*

"Good morning, Sara," he said softly, still holding me close to him.

"Good morning, Erik," I murmured into his shoulder. "Did you get some sleep?"

"I did. A few hours, but I was out like a light. You knocked me out." He grinned with *that* grin. "This coffee is helping greatly. I made it extra strong."

"Yeah, me too," I said. "On all counts. So I guess our next step is to talk to Dani, right? You first, then me. I didn't tell you that she saw us last night when we said good night. She said she's really happy, so I think that will help both our talks today."

He looked visibly relieved. "I'm glad. I know she adores you, but I wasn't sure how she'd take us being together-together."

"Together-together?" I hooted. "Is that like Facebook official?"

"Exactly," he said and kissed the top of my head. That was one of the many downsides of being short. The top of your head received all the attention. "I've got eggs ready to go in the pan. Want to join me? Dani's still sleeping."

As if on cue, my stomach growled.

"I'll take that as a yes. C'mon, I'll freshen up that coffee too. We can eat right here on the patio."

Erik held the front door for me and we made our way to the kitchen. After he showed me where things were, we weaved our way around each other as I set up a tray with utensils and napkins, salt and pepper. He was busy at the stove, scrambling the eggs and frying bacon. A full pot of coffee went on the tray also. I knew we both needed it.

"Crispy bacon, please," I called out as I carried the tray to the front door. "I mean really crispy but not burned. Because if it snaps back at me when I bite into it, I'll gag. Seriously, I'll gag."

I was out the front door before I could hear a response. I brushed some sand off the table and chairs and set the places, pouring fresh mugs of coffee. The wildflowers caught my eye and snipped a bunch with my knife. Finding a forgotten mug in the sand, I went back inside to put some water in it. I turned from the sink to see Erik grinning at me.

"What are you smiling at?" I said with a laugh.

"You. The bacon. The snap back. The gag." He cocked his head. "You make me laugh. Thank you. I needed more laughter in my life." And with that he leaned over and kissed me. He tasted decidedly like bacon. "I had to make sure it wasn't... um... snappy." His blue eyes sparkled. "It wasn't. Nice and crispy just like you like it."

Erik carried our plates out and I handled the flowers. The sky was still gray, but the air was warm, and a light breeze kept the flies to a minimum. We ate in companionable silence, the only noise coming from the waves and the gulls. I kicked off my flip-flop and rubbed my right foot against his shin under the table. When I had his full attention, I grabbed the last piece of bacon from his plate and crunched it in my mouth.

"Damn it!" he exclaimed. "I'm going to have to be much more vigilant around you, especially with food."

We sipped our coffee and refilled our mugs. Erik grabbed my hand and pressed my fingers to his mouth.

"Thank you. Thank you for coming into my world and changing it in the best way possible." He looked me up and down and waggled his brows. "And allow me to tell you how stunning you look this morning, even after ravaging me last night."

I feigned outrage. "You ravaged. You ravaged plenty, my friend." I paused and kissed him lightly. "And may I say that you are incredibly scrumptious this morning yourself."

"Why, thank you," he said. "Also allow me to commend you on the removal of the knot. Impressive."

I patted the back of my head. "It put up a good fight, but I prevailed." I winked. "I'll admit to you that the level of knottage was unsurpassed. I've never dealt with a knot that size." Punctuating my words with a blush, I remembered exactly how that knot grew to such girth. Erik picked right up on the blush, and the reason for it, and flashed that wolfish grin.

"I hope you have plenty of conditioner on hand," he stated, twirling a chunk of my hair between his fingers.

Our journey into sexy memories of the night before was interrupted by Dani coming out the front door. She was still in her pajamas, which consisted of loose shorts and a big T-shirt. Her long hair was tousled and her face still puffy with sleep. She glanced up at the gray sky and a little frown crossed her face.

"Hey, guys," Dani said, sliding into one of the patio chairs and pouring coffee into an empty mug. She looked back and forth between us with a waiting look. "Anything new I should know about?"

The latter was said with a cute little mouth twist and a mischievous twinkle in her eye. I took that moment to stand and lean down to Dani's left ear. "I'm going to go make myself busy in my own house. You guys chat. We'll talk later." Hugging her shoulders, I blew Erik a kiss and took my coffee mug back with me to the Pendleton.

Well, of course I peeked out the window of the dining room and watched Erik skootch his chair closer to Dani and take her hand. He'd come a long way in a short time. So had Dani. She looked at her father and that was the moment I wished I could read lips. I saw a lot of smiles go back and forth and a few more serious faces, but for the most part it looked like it was going well.

Taking a deep breath, I decided to be productive while they talked. I don't know why I was even a little nervous about this, but I was. Most of that was gone, and I found myself looking forward to our talk. While thoughts of last night, thoughts of Dani, and thoughts of our future ran through my head, I tidied the kitchen and poured fresh coffee. Molly was asleep in a sunbeam in the living room, and I joined her there to do some computer work.

After an hour of catching up with the Cell and letting them know that last night was *the* night, I got up and stretched and looked out the window to see if by chance Erik and Dani were still on the patio. They were. They were both sound asleep in their chairs, Erik with his head tipped straight back and his mouth wide open, and Dani with her head in her arm on the table. I snorted and called for Molly to get some fresh air.

Letting them sleep, I walked Molly down the boardwalk and noticed activity at the house on the other side of Drea's. "Looks like new neighbors, Molly. Our little patch of paradise is getting more crowded every day." I knew this was only the beginning. Once school let out, the summer people would arrive, along with the day- or week-trippers. There was a small U-Haul trailer in the driveway and I could see people moving around inside, but unfortunately, not much else, so I took my nosy arse back home to wake up the sleeping beauties. As I walked past Drea's place to the Pendleton, I noticed the redhead herself standing on her front porch. I smiled at her and said, "Good morning, Drea. How are you?"

She flicked her cold green eyes to me and gave a little huff.

"Looks like you've got Mr. Hottie McHottiepants all sewn up for yourself."

I resisted the urge to be smug and merely acknowledged her words with a nod. "Yes, we are together," I said with a shiver inside. *Together. Holy crap. We're together.*

"Lucky girl. Good thing for you that you saw him first. I totally would have moved in on that sweet piece."

I bristled slightly at her calling Erik a "sweet piece." But then I had to admit she was right, so I let it go. "Yes. Good thing for me." I changed the subject. "I see you have new neighbors coming in. With a small trailer, I doubt they're coming for a short-term rental."

Drea waved her hand nonchalantly toward her right. "Yes, I saw them arrive a little earlier. Looked like two women and a dog. A ton of luggage. They haven't unpacked the trailer yet."

I was impressed with her snooping skills. Maybe she wasn't so bad after all. But then she opened her mouth and I went back to my original analysis.

"So I guess you'll be a big part of Erik's daughter's life. Debbie? Diane? Dani. Dani's life. Listen, honey, you a mother?" she asked. I shook my head and she went on. "As the mother of a sixteen-year-old, I can be a big help to you. It's not easy raising a teenager. I might be able to give you some pointers."

Thinking back to my few encounters with Carolyn, I knew that Drea would be the last person I would ask for help. "Thanks. I'll let you know." I was tempted to add *I'll have my people call your people and we'll do lunch sometime*, but I didn't think she'd get the humor. She'd probably spend the next hour wondering who her "people" were.

I waved goodbye and headed over to Erik and Dani, both still sound asleep. Molly went straight for Erik's crotch to say good morning. "Whooooooooo." Air blew out of Erik's mouth as Molly's nose made a direct hit. Dani stirred with the commotion and I laughed at them both.

"Wake up, you guys. People are going to think you're drunk or something at eleven a.m."

They both stretched and yawned and then laughed at each other.

"Wow," Erik said. "That was a much-needed little nap."

"Lalalalala," sang Dani with her fingers stuck in her ears. "I don't want to know. It's not like I don't know, I just don't want to know. Old people sex. Ew." Then she grinned and looked at her dad. "Your turn to disappear for a while so Sara can have 'the talk' with me."

I burst out laughing. "Yeah. Time to vamoose."

Erik stood, kissed me on the lips, kissed Dani on the head, grabbed his mug, refilled it, and ambled down to the beach. The gray skies may have covered the direct sun, but it was still warm and sticky. The air down near the water would be cooler than up by the houses. "Come find me when you're done!" he called from the boardwalk.

We waved in agreement, and Dani and I looked at each other. While I knew she was happy about our change in status, her eyes showed some concern. Her serious face told me what she needed to hear.

"Dani, first off I want to assure you that I love your father. This isn't just a fling or a summer romance or cheap affair. I want to make him happy for the rest of his life."

Dani smiled and relaxed. "Dad used almost the same

words. I'm really glad you guys are together. Seriously. I always worry about him being alone. He's never had a serious relationship since Mom. He needed someone like you."

"Thank you." I said. "He's not the only one I love, you know. I'm pretty crazy about you too." Tears sprang to Dani's eyes, which made tears spring to *my* eyes. "I mean it. I've enjoyed our friendship and now it's even more special."

I continued, "I know it all happened very quickly. They always say, when you know you know. And I know. I don't know how to explain how I know, but I know." We looked at each other and burst out laughing. I waved my hands. "Oh, you know what I mean!" Which only made her laugh harder.

We wiped our tears, first from tender emotion, then from my silly ramblings. Then Dani spoke again. "I love you too, Sara. I just know this is going to be the best summer ever." Then she looked at me deadpan and in a sweet, innocent voice, she said, "Now will you tell me about that whole hair thing you had going on at four o'clock this morning?"

Holy crap. Maybe I did need to talk to Drea. "Let's go find your dad." I laughed. "Never you mind about the hair."

"Let me grab Tank. He's probably due for a walk." That sounded like a stellar idea and I ran next door and clipped the leash on Molly.

We walked down to the beach, which was almost empty on this gloomy day. Erik was easy to spot down at the water's edge. He was staring out at the horizon, the crashing of the waves covering the sound of our approach. Molly also spotted Erik and almost pulled my arm out of its socket racing toward him. I called out to Erik to try warning him, but the wind blew my words back in my face. It was an eight-foot leash. With a few feet of golden retriever attached. A golden retriever with a one-track mind. Erik. At the last moment, Molly reared up and planted both front feet on Erik's butt, throwing him forward into a well-timed, incoming wave. The wave was actually a blessing. It buffered his face-plant into the sand. I yelped, Dani yelped, and Tank sat back on the sand and watched the action unfold.

Erik bounced back up quickly, sputtering and dripping, spinning around to see what force of nature hit him. His gaze went from Molly, excited, wet, sandy, and happy, to me, wide-eyed and mouth open, to Dani, wide-eyed and looking on the verge of laughter, to Tank, butt parked in the sand nonplussed.

"I'm so—" I sputtered before Erik interrupted me.

"I'm okay. A little shaken up, but nothing's busted." He leaned down to Molly, who was wagging her tail and grinning, completely unashamed of her behavior. He ruffled her ears and looked into her eyes. "Molly. This has to stop. One of these times you are going to break my hip." He scratched her ears some more and Molly reached her face up and kissed him soundly on the nose. She decided she liked the taste of the salt water still dripping off Erik's face and proceeded to lick as much of his face as she could before he laughed and straightened up. "I needed a shower anyway," he said as he stepped toward Dani with his arms wide open. "Laughing at me, baby girl?"

Dani shrieked, knowing exactly what her father planned on doing, and jumped away, tripping over Tank sitting next to her. She tumbled in the sand, laughing hysterically. Molly figured it was time to play again and pounced on Dani.

Before it became a three-way circus, I pulled Molly away

and let Dani catch her breath. "Now both of you need a shower. And so does Molly. Which means I get another shower too."

Tank was the only one that escaped without incident. He looked pretty smug about it, too.

Everyone headed to their respective showers. After the cleansing process, Molly fell asleep on the kitchen floor and I made a cup of coffee and settled in on the couch. I must have nodded out for a little while—okay, it was forty-five minutes—when the ding from an incoming text woke me from a sweet dream involving Erik's delicious kisses.

> ERIK
> It's 3:11 p.m. I don't know how much longer I can last without kissing you. Can I come over?
>
> SARA
> I just hope you don't hit traffic on your way over here.

I heard Erik's front door slam and spotted the top of his head bobbing its way to me. When he let himself in, he found me curled up on the couch with my phone still in my hand. He sat down next to me, gently took my coffee from my other hand, and took a slow sip. Then he put it on the table and placed his hands on either side of my face and kissed me with such tenderness tears sprang to my eyes. *How could I possibly love someone so much, so fast?* After that most amazing kiss hello, he settled back on the couch and smiled at me.

"So, I think this is all going well," he stated matter-of-factly.

"Yes," I answered, giggling a little inside at his awkwardness. "Smashingly, even." That's about when the giggle slipped out.

Erik's eyes twinkled, and his eyebrow raised. "Are you mocking me?"

I placed my hands on either side of his face and kissed him every bit as tenderly as he'd kissed me moments earlier. "Yes. Yes I am."

"Ah, Sara… you are a woman of many layers. I find you irresistible. You are like this ray of sunshi—" He stopped short. "Good lord I sound like a freaking Hallmark card." He shook his head. "How did I ever write a bestseller?"

I laughed and tucked my head under his chin. "Baby, you are an amazing wordsmith. You can't be totally perfect. That would be absurd."

We both heard his front door slam and within a moment Tank walked into my living room, butt wagging. We waited, anticipating Dani to follow behind. The moments clicked by and Erik and I were sitting there with our heads cocked toward the porch. I had a visual of Tank walking himself over here, but that whole door opening opposable thumb thing kept flummoxing me.

At that moment, Dani rounded the corner and Erik and I both sat back with a little sigh. I wondered if he'd had the same visual. She was staring at her phone, open to a text message.

"Oh, hey, sorry, I was reading this text from Mom. It came in right as I walked in."

"What did your mother have to say?" Erik asked, with just the slightest edge to his voice.

Shooting him a look, she shrugged. "Not much." She read from her screen 'Having a wonderful time, just got temporary cell service. Hope you are having a good summer with your father. Love, Mom and Chris.'"

She plopped down on the couch on the other side of me. Tucking her foot under her, she leaned against me. When she put her head on my shoulder, my heart almost exploded and I melted into the couch. I leaned my head against hers. "You miss your mom. I'll bet this is hard not seeing her or having contact."

Dani sniffed a little. "Yeah. My mom has her moments, but we get along okay. She's just all wrapped up in Chris now."

Erik sat silently on my other side, watching her closely. He reached his arm over and ruffled her hair. "For what it's worth, I'm really glad you're here and I think this is going to be the best summer ever."

Dani laughed, since her dad used the same words she had earlier. "Is anyone else starving?"

Tank raised his head and I heard Molly get up in the kitchen and head to the living room. "I meant humans," she said with an eye roll. "I'm starving. Can we get a pizza or something?"

"Pizza sounds awesome!" I said, and we both looked at Erik. The dogs looked at him too.

"Do I have any choice?" Laughing, he pulled out his phone. "What kind of toppings?"

"Garbage pie!!!" Dani and I sang out in unison.

"No anchovies!" I added.

Erik dialed Lenny's Pizza and placed our order. "It's going to be about forty-five minutes," he said. "How about we take the dogs for a walk before he gets here and before it rains." He looked out the window at the ever-darkening sky.

After a stroll in the humid yet not quite drizzly late afternoon, we returned just as the pizza arrived. Erik paid the delivery kid and we entered the Pendleton to chow down. I put out some paper plates and napkins, and we opened the big square box.

We stood there staring down at the pizza, totally silent, ready to inhale sausage and pepperoni and onion and peppers, but our eyes were not looking at a garbage pie. They were looking at a Hawaiian pie. Pineapple. Blasphemy. Erik dialed Lenny's. After he hung up he said, "They mixed up two pies. Our pie is at 1135 Ocean."

We were 1131 Ocean. It must have been the new people with the U-Haul trailer. Erik closed the box with a whoosh, glanced at each of us, and said, "Let's go get our pizza."

We made it to the end of my front walk when we heard a rumble of thunder in the distance. It certainly put a pep in our step, and we did a combo of running and walking the short distance down the boardwalk to number 1135. As soon as we neared the front door, it opened and a smiling woman greeted us.

"Hi there, fellow pizza lover. We've been expecting you. I'm

Lisa. This is Tosh" she said, pointing down at her side where there was a gorgeous, black and white, mixed-breed dog. Lisa looked to be my age, with short gray hair and jeans and a T-shirt.

"I'm Rachel," said a tall, lean woman, coming into the living room from the kitchen. She finished drying her hands on a kitchen towel slung over her shoulder and stuck out her hand to each of us.

Rachel had long straight hair, a shade of dark that wasn't quite black and wasn't quite brown, but a mix in between that perfectly suited her smooth skin. She was dressed in workout clothes, and from what I could see she liked to utilize the clothes for what they were intended for. The exact opposite of why I wore them.

We introduced ourselves.

"Are you here for the entire summer?" I asked, scratching Tosh behind her ears and looking around at all the "stuff" the girls had brought with them.

"Yes and no," Lisa answered. "I own an antique shop near Philly. I'll be gone on the weekends, but Rachel will be in and out, and my son Tristan will be here every Saturday through Tuesday."

Lisa saw me glancing around and said, "I'm a leather artist. Bags, clothing, jewelry, just about anything. I want to get caught up on several commissions this summer, so I had to bring a lot of my supplies."

I felt Dani stir with interest. "I love leather stuff!" she said. "I've always wanted to try my hand at that."

"You're welcome to come over anytime." Lisa smiled at both of us. "Maybe we could all get together and create art."

"That sounds awesome," I answered for Dani and myself. "And I hate to cut this short, but both our pizzas are getting cold and the thunder is getting closer!"

A clap of thunder boomed just as I said that, making us all jump. "Yes, yes. Here." Lisa handed me our pie as Rachel took theirs from Erik. "Although you are all welcome to stay here and eat with us."

"Thank you so much, but my dog is a huge scaredy cat when it comes to thunder and I'd like to get back before the rain hits," I said ruefully, thinking how fun it would be to hang out with these women.

"Next time." She said. "You are here all summer, I trust?"

We quickly exchanged cell phone numbers, said our good-byes, and promised to see each other soon.

Back at the Pendleton with not a second to spare, we settled in with our garbage pie right as the lights flickered and went out. We all looked at each other and kept on eating.

Priorities.

A half hour later, we were happily stuffed and sitting in the living room, the generator thankfully giving us power. We ascertained the entire block as far as we could see was without power. A call to the power company confirmed that there was an outage in the area and power restoration was estimated to be within the hour. The storm rumbled outside, and Molly sat on the floor next to Dani.

I lay stretched out on the couch with my feet near Erik. Dani was on the floor absentmindedly playing with Molly's fur.

I looked from one to the other, and marveled at how much I loved having them both in my life.

"What did you think of Lisa and Rachel?" I asked.

"I liked them both from the short time we were together," Erik said. "Plus they're dog people."

I looked over at Dani. "The leatherwork interested you a lot, didn't it?"

"Oh, heck yeah. That should be fun," Dani answered, her eyes sparkling.

"I agree." I nodded. "I love being around the creative energy of other artists."

When I was about to suggest a rousing game of Go Fish, the generator shut off and I saw the streetlights blink on. Dani and Erik both sighed, I walked around and started resetting all the digital clocks.. As I got to the last clock in the kitchen, the lights went out again. I swore under my breath, tripped over a chair, and flipped the kitchen light switch on.

By the time I walked back into the living room, the lights came on again.

"Oh no. Not fooling me again. I'm parking myself right here on the couch and not resetting anything until the lights have been on for an hour." I settled back down near Erik and he grabbed one of my feet and squeezed.

"Did you trip on something in the kitchen?" he asked with an innocent smile.

I stuck my tongue out at him. He squeezed my foot again. I grinned at him. He rubbed my insole with his thumb. *Rub my feet and I'll follow you anywhere.*

"I think I'll go back to the house," Dani said, grabbing Tank's leash. Tank wasn't happy about leaving possible pizza crusts, but the call of the wild was too strong to keep him here sniffing for crumbs on my carpet. "I want to watch Netflix and Mom might try to call me tonight. I think she's supposed to be in a port somewhere today."

"Okay, kiddo," Erik said. "You know you don't have to leave, right? You okay with this?" He held up my foot.

"Holding Sara's foot?" Her eye roll practically made noise. "Please, Dad. Give me a little more credit." She gave Tank's leash a light tug. "I just feel like chilling by myself and I kinda want to be alone if Mom calls."

Pulling my foot from Erik's grasp, I got up from the couch, gave Tank a pat on the butt, and Dani a hug. "I'll see you tomorrow. Hopefully the weather will be better, and we'll get some beach time."

Dani hugged me back. Molly quickly stood and went for her leash, finally ready to go outside now that the thunder had eased as the storm passed.

"I got this," Erik said, clipping the leash to Molly's collar.

"Thanks." I smiled gratefully at him, looking around at the carnage a power outage could wreak on a living room and kitchen. "That will give me a chance to straighten up. Then we can get back to that foot rub."

With a chuckle, he walked outside with Molly into the dark, drizzly night. Later that evening, after an amazing foot rub and a few other amazing things, Erik kissed me good night and left for home.

CHAPTER 8

The next morning dawned clear and bright, no humidity, all the heavy air blown away with the storms. I yawned and stretched and was surprised to see it was only 6:30 a.m. Before showering, I decided to take Molly for a quick walk. It wasn't exactly chilly, but I put on a long-sleeved T-shirt over a tank top and yoga pants for our early morning walk. I pulled my hair into a messy bun and smoothed on some ChapStick. A pair of large sunglasses hid the lateness of the previous evening.

"C'mon girl!" I said to the sleeping pile of fur on my bed. Molly raised her head and fixed her gaze on me with a questioning look. "I don't know why I'm up so early or have this much energy, but it must be this weather, so come on, let's go for a walk." I slipped into the flip-flops next to the bed.

Molly obliged with a little grumbling, but was never one to refuse a walk. I poured a cup of coffee into a to-go mug and off we went. Erik's house was still dark and quiet, but there were a few early-morning walkers enjoying the clear morning. When I turned right onto the boardwalk, my path brought me by Drea's house first, also dark and quiet, and then Lisa's house. Which was not dark and quiet.

It had barely been light for an hour, and with the downpour the night before I wasn't sure when the girls had time to decorate the exterior of their house, but there were perfectly placed plants and flowers all around. I saw Rachel in gardening gloves and dirt-smudged, rolled-up jeans, standing barefoot in the sand, laughing at something or someone on the side deck. A few more steps showed Lisa, looking comfortable and sipping her coffee in the early morning light, wrapped in a light blanket.

"Join me!" Lisa called from her lounge chair, raising a steaming mug of coffee. I knew it was coffee because I could smell the intoxicating odor of the magic bean.

After no hesitation, Molly and I did happily join her and sank down in the soft cushions. Molly quickly found a sunbeam after I unclipped her leash and she was snoozing in no time at all.

Rachel came up on the deck, stripping off her gloves and brushing the dirt from her jeans. "Good morning." She smiled and sat down with us at the table. "It was such a beautiful morning I didn't want to waste a moment of it."

While we sipped our coffees, I learned more about Lisa and Rachel and their lives when not enjoying the Jersey shore. They'd been married for five years after meeting at the antique shop, where Rachel started visiting as a customer. Apparently, Rachel's visits became more and more frequent, and she always sought Lisa out to say hello and share a few words. Sparks flew and the rest was history. Rachel worked from home at one of those corporate jobs that I never understood no matter how much people tried to explain it to me. Her real passion was fishing and she showed us her collection of surf rods propped up against the side door.

"I had a text from Tristan a little while ago," Lisa said. "He should be here this afternoon. He mentioned a storm that might impact our weather in the next few days."

Tristan was Lisa's nineteen-year-old son, coming to stay on the weekends when she would be back home at the shop.

"Maybe I should listen to the weather report," I said, standing to leave. "I'm going to hold you to that art day you mentioned. Dani and I would love that."

Lisa laughed. "Absolutely. I'll be leaving tomorrow for home and I'll be back Sunday night. I'll text you when I get back and we'll set up some time next week, okay?"

Molly and I walked back toward home. Drea was outside sweeping sand off her front porch and I knew there was no avoiding her. I plastered a smile on my face, the "scary" one as some people referred to it. "Good morning!" I called to her.

Drea, face mostly hidden behind the largest sunglasses I'd ever seen, gave a weak smile and responded with a grimace. "Not so loud, please. It was a long night." She leaned against her broom and raised her dark sunglasses to peer at me. "I should have quit after the third Fireball, but I was having fun at the time."

I looked at her eyes, bloodshot and a bit unfocused, and almost felt sorry for her. "I'll try to keep the screaming and loud music down today," I said with a tiny bit of sarcasm. I tilted my still hot thermos of coffee at her. "Sip?"

Drea gagged a little and I wasn't sure if it was my coffee or the fact that it was *my* coffee that did it. I wished her a better day and left her still leaning on her broom. When I checked out my window five minutes later she was still standing like that. I think she may have been asleep.

I jumped in the shower after giving Molly some fresh water and breakfast. The air had warmed up by this point, so no more long sleeves for me. I pulled a sports bra from my drawer. Being on the larger size in the tata department, I was not a fan of these contraptions. There was no good way to put them on or take them off, and they created a uniboob. But the comfort level called to me, so I gave it a shot.

Just as I anticipated, I was winded merely from pulling it on over my head and getting my arms through the straps. That's where things went from bad to worse. I found myself with a tightly wrapped tube of spandex strangling my armpits and no matter how hard I tried, I couldn't get it unraveled. Couldn't get a good enough grip or the perfect angle to pull it down over the tatas. I placed both hands on my dresser and looked in the mirror. Starting to break a sweat, I looked *utterly* ridiculous—see what I did there?—stark nekkid with what looked like a hangman's noose under my arms.

Catching my breath, I considered my next step. I could text Erik to come rescue me, hoping his strong hands could unravel the dang thing, or I could wrap a towel around myself and get my scissors from the studio porch. I chose the latter. *Erik has seen enough of my disasters.* Gingerly I wrapped the towel under my arms, taking care not to add insult to injury. I slipped downstairs and out to the porch, finding my scissors on the worktable amid the mess. As I turned to go back upstairs, I heard a low whistle coming from Erik's deck.

"What are you doing, baby?" he called out. "Cutting your hair?" Damn it. He must have come out while I was showering.

Laughing as lightly as I could since deep breaths were hindered by the bra, I said "Nope, don't worry! All is fine."

He apparently took that as an invitation, because he unwound himself from his comfortable position and ambled over to my front door.

"I could never resist a woman in a towel," he murmured in my ear as he kissed me good morning. He pulled the towel away from my chest even though I was gripping it tightly over the bound-up bra. His lips moved down my neck, softly whispering lovely nothings as his soft lips kissed every inch on their way down toward my breastbone. When his mouth reached the bra, he paused, and I waited for the question.

"Um, Sara?" Erik's eyebrows were raised. "Problem?" Obviously, he had come to his own conclusions based on the evidence of spandex and scissors.

"Just never mind!" I laughed. "Forget you ever saw this."

His shoulders shaking with laughter, and his eyes filled with unshed tears, he choked out, "Are you actually so stuck in your bra that you're going to cut your way out?"

I put my nose up in the air and sniffed. "Why yes, yes I am." And I turned to go back upstairs to the privacy of the bathroom to attempt my great bra escape. Remembering too late that Erik had a grip on my towel, I was minus one towel by the time I reached the doorway from the porch to living room. Dropping my chin, I hung my head and put my hand out, offering him the scissors.

A soft chuckle escaped his lips as he took the shears from me. "Do you want me to try unraveling this or just cut your losses?"

"Just cut the freaking thing off me, please," I begged. "I can hardly take a deep breath."

The bra came off with a few crunches of the scissors. The relief was blessedly quick. I gulped in oxygen like I had been tumbling in the waves and broke through the water to the sweet, life-giving air. Erik watched me with controlled amusement. I grabbed the towel from his shoulder and tried to grab some dignity. "Thank you," I said seriously. "I'll be right back."

He made a strangled noise and I tried not to make eye contact with him but failed. His eyes were ripped wide open and his lips were pressed tightly together. If I had to guess, I'd say his cute butt cheeks were clenched just as tightly. I realized the ridiculousness of the situation. I also realized there was only one way of handling it. A giggle left my lips and that was only the beginning. At once, Erik relaxed everything, letting his building laughter out.

We stood there on the porch, me draped in a towel, Erik holding me in a bear hug while we cackled and chortled and snickered for about five minutes. Finally, I wiped the tears of laughter from my face, sniffed loudly, and told him I'd be back after regrouping.

"Hang on," he said in a husky voice, grabbing my arm before I could slip completely from his arms. "Thank you."

"For what?" I asked.

"For being you. For making me laugh every single day

since I met you. For seeing me. For letting me see you." He paused, searching for words. "I feel like life has more color now. Like the future's so bright I need to wear shades." And then he stopped talking and his eyes got really big again.

"Did you just choke and use eighties song lyrics?" I gasped.

"Yes," he admitted in a strangled voice, "but I used better grammar."

I lost it again. Shaking my head, laughter once again erupting, I choked out, "I love you too, baby" and ran upstairs.

Dani wandered over as I reappeared downstairs, composed, dressed, and ready to attack the day. "Hi, Sara, is my dad over here?"

"He was before I went upstairs to get changed. Let me check the kitchen." I also looked in the bathroom and out the back window but didn't see Erik anywhere. "Not here," I said, returning to her.

We both looked around the living room, and then Dani laughed and pointed out the window, looking toward Drea's house next door. There stood Erik talking to Drea, or perhaps I should say "listening" to Drea. He had that pained look on his face again, but I'm sure not for the same reasons.

"Should we rescue him?" Dani asked.

"Probably."

"Right now, or should we torture him for a minute?" she asked with a giggle.

I managed to put a disapproving look on my face and clicked my tongue. "I'm disappointed."

"Rescue him?" she asked with a surprised look on her face.

"Oh, gosh no. This is way too good. A minute is too short. I wonder if I have popcorn," I responded.

Giggling, Dani threw her arms around me and hugged me. I hugged her back, smiling into her shoulder at how much I loved this girl. We crouched in sync at the window, trying to be inconspicuous. We did very poorly at this, and Erik spotted us over Drea's shoulder. I waved my fingers at him. He shook his head ever so slightly.

"I think he's scared we'll make him laugh," I said to Dani.

"Like we'd ever do that."

"Never," I continued the lie.

As if we had ESP, and perhaps we did, we raised our thumbs to our ears and wiggled our fingers and stuck out our tongues.

It would have been hysterically funny watching Erik trying to hold himself together, except Drea was watching Erik's eyes and realized his attention was not on her or her attributes. That's when she turned around to see what captured his attention and saw the two of us playing monkey.

Dani and I dropped out of sight and laughed until we cried. I'd laughed so much already today that my cheeks hurt. We peeked up over the sill and Erik and Drea were still standing there staring at our window.

"Sorry!" I called out, waving. "We were just being silly to Erik." Drea smiled, and even though she was still wearing the oversized sunglasses, I knew it didn't reach her icy eyes. She gave a slight wave and turned her full attention back to Erik.

A few minutes later, Erik found Dani and me in the kitchen eating gelato straight from the container. "You guys are a dangerous duo." He laughed. "I'm in deep doo-doo with the two of you teaming up."

We smiled in unison, our mouths full of salted caramel deliciousness.

"I was craving popcorn, but this will do," I said. "What are the plans for the day?"

It was still early—this waking up with the sun stuff had its perks.

"Well, I'm heading to a meeting, which I wish Drea would consider," he said with a frown. "She was hungover and I'm not sure if the smell of alcohol was fresh or still hanging from last night."

I rubbed his arm. "Yeah, I spoke to her earlier. She was in rough shape."

"I stepped out while you were changing, with the intention of getting Tank, but she spotted me and called me over," he explained. "She just wanted to complain about her headache and ask that I not pound nails or run saws today."

"What did you say back?" Dani asked.

"Well, it took her a few minutes to get to her request and right as she finished, I saw the two of you knuckleheads at the window." He laughed. "I told her I'd be happy to take a break today, but tomorrow I'm back at it."

"Any sign of Carolyn?" I asked, curious about the vampirish girl.

"She's not there. Drea mentioned that Carolyn left yesterday to spend the summer with Drea's mother in Brooklyn."

I raised my eyebrows. "That didn't last long."

"Apparently there's 'too much sun' here. She couldn't

handle it," he continued. "Maybe that's why Drea tied one on last night."

"Maybe," I said, a little relieved I wouldn't have to pry conversation out of Carolyn. "So that leaves the dangerous duo alone and unsupervised while you're out." I glanced over at Dani.

She smiled. "Beach?"

"Why not?" I said. "It definitely warmed up enough. Oh, we're going to have an art day with Lisa soon."

Dani jumped up and down excitedly. "I can't wait!"

"Also, Lisa's son is arriving tonight or tomorrow. He'll be coming and going for the summer," I explained. "He's at the shop while Lisa is here. Lisa mentioned it when we exchanged the pizzas." My mind fumbled for his name.

"Tristan," Dani said, perking up. "How old is he? Did Lisa say?"

Erik's head shot up at the eagerness in Dani's voice. "Son? She mentioned a son?"

Ignoring Erik, I answered, "Nineteen."

Erik laughed. "Oh, great. I'm looking at quite a summer ahead of me, aren't I?"

Dani laughed, Erik groaned, and I clucked my tongue at Molly since it was time for a walk.

CHAPTER 9

Molly and I returned from our walk to find Dani sitting on one of the Adirondack chairs in my front yard. It was a "yard" in name only—the grass was nonexistent other than the tall beach grass that grew along the small dune between my house and Erik's. She had already changed into a bikini, neon green, and a cute white oversized tank top as a cover. Dani's hair was pulled up in a messy bun. Without a stitch of makeup and a rosy glow to her skin, she looked happy and relaxed. *What a change from the first time I saw her.*

"Give me five minutes and I'll join you. Help yourself to water if you want one," I said as Molly and I walked by.

Dani responded by pulling a stainless steel water bottle from her beach bag. "I'm all set. Water, magazines, sunscreen."

After making sure Molly had fresh water, I went upstairs and changed into a black one-piece suit, still sexy but with more area covered. Pulling my hair into a bun like Dani's, I applied sunscreen all over and slipped my feet into black flip-flops. Before going downstairs, I visited the bathroom and remembered why I hate one-piece swimsuits so much.

Once everything was tucked back in place, I went downstairs and filled a water bottle. Molly was asleep on a shady part of the carpet and I ruffled her ears. "You be a good girl." She thumped her tail on the carpet in response. My beach bag was prestocked with magazines, one of Erik's bestsellers, and a couple of packages of almonds in case the hungries hit. I added the bright blue water bottle and went outside to where Dani awaited my arrival.

Dani let out a whoop and jumped to her feet. That was no easy feat from an Adirondack chair. A move like that would throw my back out for a month. "Let's beach it!" she called out over her shoulder as she skipped to the boardwalk ahead of me.

I laughed. "I'll find you. I'm sure the beach is pretty empty. Go ahead and pick the perfect spot."

Dani did as I instructed and by the time I got there she had her towel laid out and was already on her stomach, reading a magazine under her crossed arms. I spread my towel next to hers and set up my beach chair next to that. I was correct in my assumption that the beach would be empty. A couple of fishermen, their poles stuck down in the sand by the water, were watching their lines from beach chairs nearby. There were maybe ten people total enjoying the sunshine with us on this gorgeous day.

I settled into my chair and opened the paperback novel written by the man I was falling deeply in love with. It had made the bestseller list about fifteen years earlier, but I'd never had the chance to read it. I checked out the photo on the back of the book. It differed from the one I'd seen on his newer hardcover, which stood on my shelf. A younger, tenser Erik stared back at me. Still dressed casually in tight jeans and a denim shirt, the biggest difference was the length of his hair—much longer in the younger photo—and the not-quite-a-smile purse of his lips.

"That's an old picture of dad from when I was a little girl."

I started, not realizing Dani had raised up on an elbow to see what I was looking at.

Laughing at my jumpiness, she continued, "My mom took that picture. It was right before they split up. You can see how unhappy my dad looks there."

"He's certainly not smiling. He almost has an annoyed look on his face," I replied.

"I was too little to realize how unhappy they both were, but I remember a lot of silences in my house. There wasn't a lot of yelling, but there wasn't a lot of laughing either. Even though I was only four, I remember the silence when they were both in the same room."

I reached over and rubbed her back a little. "It must have been a very tough time."

"It's really all I've ever known, so I'm okay with it. I'd rather they both be happy with other people if they can't be happy together. And they are." She smiled as she said the last words. "Do you think you and Dad will get married?"

After I choked on my own saliva, I raised my sunglasses and looked at her face, expecting to see a teasing look. But I saw a hopeful look instead. "It's a little early to even think about that."

"I'm just thinking that both of you are… um…"

"Old?" I queried, my eyebrows up around my hairline somewhere.

Dani hooted, "No! Not old. Just older. You know, not younger." She took a long sip of water from her bottle while she let me process that.

I thought back to the fifty-somethings who were in my life when I was sixteen. *They were ancient,* whispered my inner truth teller. "You're being kind. Believe it or not, even when you're older, you still think you're young. So, it's okay. You'll get there one day, and you'll understand."

"I don't think you're old at all, Sara," Dani insisted. "But I think you should make the most out of every day and not waste a second."

"How'd you get so wise, little girl?" I asked.

She merely smiled in response and we both went back to our reading.

After a few hours of sun, sand, and salt water, we picked up our towels and bags, I grabbed my chair, and we headed back to the house.

"I'm surprised Dad didn't come find us after his meeting," she said.

"Me too," I replied. "Probably working on the house or writing. Taking advantage of the quiet." I winked as I said the last part.

Dani laughed. "He'd better get used to the noise!"

We stepped off the beach onto the boardwalk and saw Erik sitting on the front deck talking to Drea. They had mugs of what I assumed was coffee in front of them. Erik was speaking earnestly and Drea listened with her arms crossed over her chest. I knew enough about body language that the arms-crossing thing meant she wasn't willing to listen. It also meant that her double Ds were squished and overflowing her halter top sundress. Erik seemed to be doing a good job of keeping his eyes focused on her glittering green ones and not on anything south of her chin.

He saw us approaching and waved us over.

"We don't want to intrude on anything…" I said, my voice trailing off.

"Nope! It's cool, we're just shooting the breeze," he said, with a look of relief.

Drea shifted in her chair, slowly lifted her mug to her full pouty lips, and smiled before taking a sip. Dani bristled beside me. She wasn't exactly standing close enough for me to physically feel the bristle, but I could feel the tension surrounding her.

"I'm going to shower and change," Dani muttered as she walked past us into the house.

"Moody teens," Drea said. "There were days I could hardly get one word out of Carolyn. She's gone back to New York to stay with my mother, by the way." She paused and looked at me. "I wasn't sure if Erik mentioned that to you."

Like they had some long, secret conversation. "Yes, he did tell me. I hope she'll be happier there than here with all this sun and sand."

Drea dropped her gaze, and I had a momentary pang of guilt for my comment. I say momentary because when she raised her eyes again, they were focused on Erik. She pouted her lips and rested her hand on Erik's arm. "Can we continue this again soon? I have more questions." Fluttering her eyelashes, she took a deep breath and slowly let it out.

Erik had a bemused look on his face and said, "Of course. I have lots of answers, and if I don't, someone I know will."

Drea stood, smoothing down the folds of her dress and offering Erik one last look at her attributes. To his credit, he kept his eyes trained on hers. Drea blew him a kiss and waved her fingers at me. Her smile may not have reached her eyes, but the challenge in them came through loud and clear.

I raised my eyebrows and hopefully my steady gaze back to her said, *Game on, bitch.* I'm not sure if that's what came through, but her eyebrows shot up, so I took that as mission accomplished. I was fully prepared to mark my territory against this viper, and I chuckled at the mental picture of me peeing a circle around Erik. "Enjoy your evening, Drea," I murmured as she walked by me. There was no response forthcoming and I watched her sashay away toward her house.

"What the heck just happened?" Erik asked. "I felt like she was coming on to me hot and heavy for a few minutes there." He shook his head slowly. "I was trying to talk to her about alcohol and possibly coming to a meeting, and she was asking a few questions about AA. I thought I was making a little progress and then BAM she started shutting down and acting strange."

"Right around the time Dani and I exited the beach," I said, nodding wisely. "She's got an agenda, Erik. Please be aware of that. I understand you want to help someone in distress, and I respect the hell out of you for that. But keep in the back of your mind that she wants you."

He touched my cheek softly with the back of his hand. "I know, baby. Well aware. I've met plenty of Dreas in my lifetime. Will you trust me that I can handle this?"

I looked deep into his eyes and felt the power of his earnest gaze. *Do I trust him? How long have I known him? What if he's a player? How would I even know?* I pushed the thoughts out of my mind. *I'd know—*

Erik interrupted my inner conversation. "Sara?" His eyebrows were raised so high they disappeared into the tousled hair hanging down on his forehead, and the concern in his eyes cemented my belief that he was telling me the truth. I wasn't some naive kid and I'd never sent money to a Nigerian prince or to a Facebook scammer, so I was feeling pretty sure of myself and my ability to read people.

I grinned up at him and lightly kissed his lips, running my fingertips over his forehead and smoothing down his worry lines. "I believe you," I assured him, and for a few minutes we were lost in each other's arms and lips.

When we were done making out in full view of the world —*oh please, let Drea be watching*—I told Erik I was going to take Molly for a quick walk and then shower. Regretfully I broke out of our embrace and walked next door. Before entering the porch, I turned to blow a kiss at Erik, totally mimicking Drea's earlier farewell, but I saw he wasn't looking at me. His eyes were trained on the house next door, and more specifically on Drea, standing on her front porch staring back at him. I was a little too far away to see the look on her face, but her pose was provocative, back curved, boobs a'poppin'. Frozen, I stood there for a moment, a million thoughts running through my head, most of which involved me kicking ass.

Molly's quick bark from inside roused me from my fantasy and I opened the porch door. Before I could step onto the porch, Molly bolted past me down the front walk, turned right, and took off down the boardwalk. Erik and I screamed, "Molly!" at the same time, and I took off running down the walk in my bathing suit, gauzy cover-up, and flip-flops. Erik sprinted from his front yard to mine and took off diagonally, overtaking me in short order. Drea watched from her front porch with her hands clasped over her open mouth and I wasn't quite sure whether she was feigning concern or laughing at the sight of me running. I almost had to give her that—it wasn't pretty.

Dani, overhearing the yells for Molly, came running out of the house and joined the chase.

I was scared to death that Molly would run down one of the side streets that met the boardwalk and reach the highway. My heart was pounding out of my chest, both from the exertion of running barefoot—I'd kicked off my flip-flops a block earlier—and from fear. Molly was not prone to running off. I remember only a couple of times and both involved a deer, a field, and a frisbee. The breakout happened so quickly I never saw what caught Molly's attention on the nearly deserted boardwalk.

Erik was ahead of me by a block. I could see him easily jogging to the entrance of each side street and looking toward the highway, then continuing the jog. Dani was half a block ahead of me looking in yards and at sand dunes. I was gasping for air by this point, my short legs unable to keep up, and the support in a bathing suit was nothing to brag about. I stopped running and walked over to a bench. Tears burned behind my eyelids. *We'll find her. We'll find her.* A new thought crossed my mind. *What if she ran onto the beach?* After checking that Erik and Dani were still ahead and hadn't found her, I hauled myself off the bench and took the next entrance to the beach. The late-afternoon sun glinted off the waves, light and rippling in low tide. I cupped my hands over my eyes and scanned the beach to the left. Nothing except some fishermen and surfers awaiting the soon incoming high tide. I checked the waves on the outside chance she jumped into the ocean, my stomach clenching with this new anxiety. Nothing except the diamonds of sunlight on the water. I scanned to my right and saw something several hundred yards ahead moving at a fast clip and too low to be human. Also, humans don't have tails wagging that fast.

I swallowed a sigh of relief and screamed, "Molly!" to which there was no response. She was too far away, and the ocean sounds drowned out my screams. I ran back up onto the boardwalk and yelled for Dani, the closer of the two. She finally turned around and I waved my arms wildly and pointed to the beach. Luckily, she understood my *land the plane arms* and yelled to her father ahead, doing the same actions. All three of us entered the beach at the entrance closest to where we were and took off down the beach as fast as we could, calling for Molly. I could still see her, dancing in and out of the waves and then running away as Erik drew closer. *She thinks we're playing with her.*

"Wait!" I croaked out, truly believing my lungs were going to explode. "Stop!"

Erik and Dani stopped running and dropped down to the sand, both breathing heavily. I caught up to them after a moment and dropped down beside them, all of us sweating

SUMMER OF SARA

and worn out and now covered with sand. A lump formed in my throat and a tear escaped my eye. "Damn it, Molly…"

Erik put a sandy hand on my knee. "She'll tucker out soon and come back. Any idea what she went after?"

I shook my head no and told them that it all happened too quickly. I never noticed anything.

The three of us sat there for a few minutes, watching Molly prance around and greet the few people on the beach. They looked around to find the dog's owner and before they could grab her collar, she ran off again. Dani got up and tried to walk quickly toward the soaking wet golden retriever. Unfortunately, every time Dani would get within twenty feet of Molly, the dog would take off running in the opposite direction. Dejected, Dani walked back to where we were still catching our breath.

"Maybe we should try to corral her. It'll be easier to run on the boards, so I'll run ahead and get in front of her. You and Dad take the beach and we'll surround her as well as we can."

Erik and I looked at each other. "She gets her brilliance from me, of course," he said with an innocent look on his face. I snorted in response and Dani ran to the boardwalk entrance after judging how far down Molly had gotten. Erik stood up and reached a very welcome hand down to help me up. We walked quickly toward Molly; running in the sand was beyond us both. I stripped off my cover-up while we walked and took a detour into the ocean, gasping as the water hit my overheated body. I dove into a small wave, got my hair wet, and walked back to Erik.

"Much better," I said, refreshed and ready for battle.

Erik decided I was brilliant also and ran into the water in his cutoffs and T-shirt. I scanned the beach ahead and spotted

Molly with a young man in the distance. He had her by the collar and he was looking around the beach for who belonged to the dog. Molly was sitting nicely, her tail wagging and spraying sand around her. When we were still two blocks away from them, I spotted Dani coming onto the beach directly in their path. She clapped her hands and said something, but we were too far away to hear her. We waved and the three of us descended on the young man and the wet dog.

Dani was first to reach them, and I saw her bend down and ruffle Molly's fur. I watched as she looked up at the young man and smiled. When we finally got to them, Dani and the young man were still smiling at each other. "Molly. Seriously. What the hell," I scolded my girl at the same time I hugged her. Molly responded with more tail wags, a huge grin, and a big kiss on my cheek.

"Thank you *so* much. We couldn't get her to stop and you were in the right place at the right time. Thank you," I babbled on a bit in my relief. Erik waved his sandy hand and thanked him. Dani was still standing in the same spot with the same smile on her face. I looked at him more closely. *Very cute. Dark hair, twentyish, slender but muscular. Great teeth.* I could see his great teeth because, after responding humbly to our thanks, his attention turned back to Dani and his smile matched hers.

Erik and I looked at each other. We were still wet from our quick dip, my cover-up on backward, my flip-flops long ago discarded, his clothes plastered to him and his hair almost as wild as mine. At the same time, we pointed at each other and started laughing. Which made us laugh even harder.

Dani and the smiling guy looked at us like we were weird, and I suppose we appeared a bit ridiculous. I moved past the awkward moment and stuck my hand out. "Hi, I'm Sara, this is Erik, and this is Dani. Oh, and this pile of wet fur is Molly."

"Tristan. Nice to meet you guys. I just got here, and I was taking a walk to check the beach out. Glad I could help," he said, tentatively sticking his hand out to shake Erik's sandy, wet one.

"That's okay," Erik said, holding his hands up. "I wouldn't want to shake my hand right now. So, Tristan was it? Any possibility you're Lisa's son?"

Tristan's eyebrows shot up in surprise. "Yes! How did you know?"

"The name isn't that common, and we knew you might be arriving today. We're practically neighbors and met your mom and Lisa the other day."

"Cool." Tristan said. "Are you guys a family?" he asked, waving his finger between Erik, Dani, and me.

For some unknown reason I chose that moment to blush deep purple and stammered, "N-no. We're dating. And Dani is Erik's daughter. We live next door to each other."

Tristan nodded wisely and glanced back at Dani who was still in the same position and still smiling. I watched the sparks fly and knew weekends with my favorite girl would soon be limited.

"Let's get Molly home so I can get us showered," I said to Erik.

Dani and Tristan followed behind us, making small talk and getting to know each other. Erik threw a sandy arm around my shoulders and kissed the top of my sandy head. I smiled up at the specks of sand left on his lips and tucked my head into his chest. We awkwardly walked like that over the uneven sand until I started tipping over sideways. Erik caught me before I hit the sand and he chuckled as I blushed. Dani stifled a giggle and I turned my head and stuck my tongue out at her, which only made her giggle more. Tristan wisely kept his face neutral and the four of us continued our long walk back to the Pendleton.

When we finally got back home, I left Erik, Dani, and Tristan to talk to Drea who must have been watching from her window and ran out as we walked past. I took Molly directly to the outdoor shower to try to rinse off the sandy tangles, scolding her gently about taking off. Once I had Molly taken care of and tied outside to dry, I stripped and showered off the ravages of the afternoon. Once again, I thanked the Gods of Outdoor Showers. Of course, the challenge was to remember to bring a towel with you, and it only took me two times to forget before I always made sure there was a spare in the shower stall. I made use of that spare towel and ran inside to get dressed. It was still quite warm, even though it was close to dinnertime, so I chose a sundress that skimmed my knees with a tight bodice that accentuated my curves. The deep green color brought out my tan and I twirled in front of the mirror and laughed. I was feeling good. I was newly in love with a pretty spectacular guy who also happened to love me, and I adored his daughter. The prospect of the summer ahead made me twirl until I collapsed on the bed in a dizzy heap.

Once the room stopped spinning I addressed my hair and makeup. I wasn't sure what our plans were for tonight, but I wanted to look as good as I felt. Glancing out the window, I noticed Tristan and Dani had disappeared, but Erik was still talking to Drea. I calculated that I'd been inside at least thirty minutes. *That's a lot of talking.* Drea's head was down and her shoulders were slumped. I could see Erik's lips move as he spoke to her, and Drea kept shaking or nodding her head in response. Finally, Erik patted her on the shoulder and walked away and up the walk to my house. I watched Drea's eyes follow him as he walked, her eyes narrowed and her chin jutted out.

Erik let himself in as I came downstairs to the living room. "Hey you, I just wanted to let you know I'm going to jump in the shower and hit another meeting. Drea has asked if I'd take her to one. The church in Seaside has a 6:00 p.m. on Fridays, so we'll head down there."

I swallowed down the feeling of jealousy. Who was I to question someone wanting help with alcohol? Unfortunately, I still believed Drea had an agenda to fulfill and if it took using her drinking to achieve that agenda, she'd gladly use it. "Sure, no worries." I said. "I'm glad she's at least open to talking about it." I made a vow to keep my friends close and my enemies closer. I'd told Erik I trusted him and that I believed that he could handle Drea's attentions, but I still held a tiny little seed of doubt. Like any other woman, I could be a little stubborn about letting go. "Is Dani with Tristan?"

"No, she's in the house. Tristan went back to his mom's," Erik said. "I should be home by seven thirty. How about I drop Drea off and then you, me, and Dani head down to the Crab's Claw for dinner?" He paused for a moment, taking me in with his eyes. "Sara, you look gorgeous. How did I get so lucky?"

I grinned up at him, snaking my arms around his neck and drawing his lips down to mine. I know my kiss answered his question, because after we stopped to take a breath, he gave a contented sigh and kissed the top of my head. "I hope you have a great meeting, and I hope Drea sees the light. I think I'll catch up on some computer stuff, bills, and whatnot until you get back. Tell Dani to come over if she doesn't feel like being alone."

Erik agreed and set off across the sand that separated our two homes. I watched him walk away from me with mixed emotions. *Stop assuming things*, I told myself. *You're assuming Drea is a predator, so you're experiencing self-doubt and jealousy and there's no room in your life for this.* I spoke very sternly with myself, hoping I'd listen.

CHAPTER 10

A few minutes before 6:00 p.m., I peeked out my window and the peek just happened to be in the direction of Drea's house. I watched as she walked down her front steps, heading to the boardwalk. Swaying down the boardwalk past my house, she headed for Erik's. She raised her gaze to my front porch, where I happened to be standing, and she gave me her frosty smile and a little wave. And I watched myself wave back with a matching icy smile.

She was dressed in a cute sundress much like the cute sundress I had on. Except with her height and long legs, she looked like a Victoria's Secret model. She was made up and her hair perfectly beach tousled. As she approached Erik's front door, her hips started swaying a little harder. Tank barked from inside Erik's house, and Drea faltered a bit in her sway. The front door opened, and Erik came out, looking gorgeous as always in a nicely fitting pair of jeans and a T-shirt, his hair still wet from his shower. Drea's eyes were glittering. From thirty feet away, I could see glittering. Smiling with all her teeth showing, she didn't look at all like a woman going through any kind of crisis. As they walked away from where I was standing, Drea looked over her left shoulder at my front porch. And then she winked and waved.

I stewed for about thirty seconds after they left for the meeting. This was on me. My own insecurities were making the butterflies in my stomach go berserk. But I also knew what some women were capable of. *Until Drea actually makes a move, let it go,* said the little voice in my head. And even if she did make a move, I needed to trust that Erik would rebuff her advances.

I was standing in the same position a few minutes later when Dani came out with Tank and headed over to my front door. "Hey," I said, glad to have a distraction from my own brain.

"Hey." Dani said. I noticed a little extra eye makeup and a pretty shade of pink gloss on her lips.

"I know that's not for me," I said, pointing at her face. "Hot date?"

She blushed almost as pink as her lip gloss. "Tristan said he'd be walking the boards tonight and asked if I'd like to get ice cream. I asked Dad before he left, and he said it was okay as long as we kept to the boards and weren't alone in the house at any point." She smoothed down the T-shirt she was wearing over her denim cutoffs and futzed with her hair for a moment before continuing, "He's really cute, isn't he Sara?"

"Indeed," I responded. "And you look amazing. Any guy would be lucky to have you on his arm. Make sure he treats you nicely. I have a feeling your dad would not be happy if he found out otherwise." I cocked an eyebrow at her. "And neither would I."

Dani hugged me and promised she'd be cautious. "He seems really nice. We talked for a while after you went in this afternoon."

"Does he know how old you are?"

"Yup. He asked me, and I told him I was a month away from turning seventeen. He's nineteen. That's not a big age difference, right?"

"The big difference is that he's over eighteen and you're not." I laughed. "So just be careful and have fun."

"I get it. I promise," she said. "Hey, did you see that Drea went to a meeting with Dad?"

"I saw," I said flatly.

My tone must have caught Dani's attention and she glanced at me with a teasing look. "She was all prettied up. I could still smell her perfume by the front door and they left ten minutes ago. But you're prettier, Sara. Much prettier. And nicer. You're real and funny."

I hugged her again. "Thanks. Yeah, I was a little jealous. I'll admit it. Something about that woman…" My voice trailed off.

Molly and Tank chose that moment to play zoomies and if you've never seen a golden retriever and a bulldog playing zoomies together, your life is lacking. Dani and I laughed at the dogs for a few minutes until they tuckered themselves out and ended up in the kitchen, drinking water, taking turns until they drank their fill.

"I'm taking Molly for a walk to kill some time until your dad gets back," I told Dani, dismissing the little voice in my head reminding me about the computer work and bills. I was too distracted to work on anything important. "Do you want to come, or are you on Tristan watch?"

"I'll come with you," she said, clipping the leash back on Tank. "Tristan said around seven or seven thirty."

I glanced at the clock on my cell phone and saw it was only 6:20 p.m. "We'll take a long, slow walk while we wait for our menfolk."

Dani snorted. "Menfolk? What are we, like ninety?"

I lightly yanked a lock of her long hair. "Tread lightly, little girl." I laughed. "Don't forget, I'm a woman on edge."

We bantered back and forth as we walked north on the boardwalk, teasing each other about the male species as the sun set, giving off the most magnificent light of the day.

"Photographers call this 'The Golden Hour.' It's a popular time of day to shoot," I told Dani.

We paused at one of the decks jutting out over the sand dune. Pulling our cell phones out, we snapped pictures of the sea, the beach and its few occupants, the dogs, and finally each other. After a few selfies together, we sat on the bench and enjoyed the magical light. The dogs settled at our feet and I started feeling better about the whole Drea thing. *Everything is going to be okay.* Lather, rinse, repeat.

Erik was at my front door by twenty past seven and gave me a huge hug upon entering. "I missed you," he said quietly. "And can I ask a weird question? How do you get the smell of someone's perfume out of your nose? It's stuck there."

"I missed you too. Probably the only way to get rid of it is to take your girlfriend to the Crab's Claw and fill your sinuses with the smell of snow crab clusters and melted butter."

Erik laughed and drew me back into a tight embrace. "I love you, Sara. Have I told you that today?"

"Not nearly enough." I smiled. "I hope it went okay." I knew better than to ask for details about the meeting, knowing Erik couldn't and wouldn't answer. "Dani just took off for a walk with Tristan. She brought Tank along, kind of a quasi-chaperone."

"So we're alone?" He said with a naughty glint in his eye. "Too bad I made reservations." He slid a finger from my bottom lip, down my chin and neck, to the small bit of cleavage my dress exposed.

The warm rush from my center expanded to my fingers and toes. This man knew all my good pushable buttons. I grabbed his finger from its travels and lightly bit his fingertip. "Feed me first, baby, then we won't have to worry about any reservations." I gave him my naughtiest smile and prayed it didn't come off like one of the dental patients with a numb lip.

We were both chuckling as we walked the few blocks to the restaurant, hand in hand. The evening was warm and still light, many of the homes lit as the summer people were slowly arriving, allowing me to look in the windows. I loved looking at how other homes were decorated, always ready for new ideas at my condo. I shook my head gently at the thought of my pretty little condo, not wanting to think about life after September yet. It was too new, too soon to start projecting what our future held together. I knew I loved him and wanted him in my life until my last breath. The questions of logistics would come later.

A line had formed outside the restaurant, but we were ushered to our seats after only a few minutes. The waiter took our drink order, unsweetened iced tea for us both, and left us perusing the menu. There was no question what I wanted, snow crab having been on my mind since Erik mentioned dinner out. Erik decided on lobster tail. As we waited for our dinners, I took a deep breath and casually asked him if Drea was okay.

His eyes darkened a bit. "I'm not really sure what's going on with Drea. I can't tell you specifics, but there's just something about her…"

Funny how our voices trailed off as we tried to put our finger on what that something was.

"I won't ask. I wouldn't do that. And I hope she gets the help she's looking for," I said. "Do you think she'll attend another meeting?"

"Oh, that one I can answer. Yes. As a matter of fact, I wanted to talk to you about exactly that. On Sunday there's a 9:00 a.m. meeting here in Lavallette. My sponsee has chosen that meeting to celebrate and the meeting is 'open' which means anyone can come. Lots of people bring family and loved ones to witness the ceremony. I'll be presenting him with his thirty-day coin. I want you and Dani to come," he said. "It would mean a lot to me."

"Of course, I'll be there. I'm sure Dani will too. I went to my brother's celebrations, and they are special meetings." I paused for a moment and asked, "What does that have to do with Drea?"

"We talked about sobriety dates and I mentioned my sponsee was celebrating this Sunday. She said she wanted to be there."

That was the moment I discovered how hard it is to suppress an eye roll. "I'm sorry," I said. "That eye roll was uncalled for. I still think she has an agenda, but I want to give her the benefit of the doubt."

"I know. Trust me, I get it. But let's not talk about Drea anymore tonight. I'm just starting to get her perfume out of my nostrils."

We clinked our iced teas, and the waiter appeared with our meals. A massive platter of snow crab clusters sat in front of me. A decent-sized lobster tail adorned Erik's plate. Large bowls of melted butter and a bowl of lemon wedges soon joined them. Fresh, warm rolls and a large bowl for discarded crab shells completed the table. The waiter handed Erik a lobster bib and he put it on, his face revealing a bit of discomfort.

"You look very handsome with your bib," I teased. "Hang on while I take your picture."

Before I could reach for my phone, Erik started laughing and grabbed my hand. "Not a chance. Besides, if you wait till the end of the meal, you can get one with butter smeared all over my face and lobster stuck in my teeth."

"True," I said. "Thanks for pointing that out." Everything was going along fine until I started cracking a crab leg in front of me, trying as always to get the piece of meat to slide out in one hunk. It was a challenge every time and one I believed I had cultivated to a fine art. I picked up my little crab fork and worked the tasty treat out of the shell slowly so as not to tear the flesh. It hung up at the end, and I gave it a small tug. That's when it slid completely out of the shell, flew across the table, and landed on Erik's lap. He looked down, looked at me, and looked down again.

I slowly wiped my mouth with a napkin. "Um, whoops?" I said, trying not to laugh. Erik reached down, and his hand came back up with the still intact crab meat. He stared at me, dunked the leg into his butter, and sucked the whole thing into his mouth.

"My lap, my crab," he said.

I couldn't argue with that.

After dinner we sat back in our chairs, stuffed to the gills. Pun intended. Erik patted his belly and let out a moan of contentment. "Perfect dinner, perfect dinner companion, perfect evening."

The waiter approached to take our empty platters and asked about dessert.

"Nothing for me. I'm so full. But please get something if you want it," I said to Erik.

He agreed with me and asked the waiter for the check. I offered to pay half or leave the tip, but Erik waved my words away. We left the restaurant and decided to walk back on the boardwalk since we'd walked on the main street to get there. The sun had set, and a breeze had picked up, causing me to shiver slightly in my sleeveless dress. Noticing the shiver, he put his arm around me as we made our way home. We'd walked about a block on the boards, when I noticed a couple several yards ahead of us.

I poked Erik. "Hey, is that Dani and Tristan ahead of us?" In the growing darkness I couldn't be sure but then focused on the dog walking ahead of them. "It is!" I whispered. "There's Tank. Let's catch up to them."

Erik's arm tightened around my shoulders. "Let's not be so hasty. I'd like to just hang back and watch for a couple of blocks."

We picked up our pace a bit to get a little closer without being noticed. Luckily a few other people were walking the boards, most of them holding ice-cream cones. There was an excellent ice cream shop a block past the restaurant. I shivered at the thought of ice cream. Erik's arm wasn't exactly a warm sweater. At my shiver, his arm tightened, and he rubbed his hand up and down my arm. I glanced up at him, squirming as his fingertips found my goose bumps.

"Are these all over your body, Sara?" He flashed that wolf smile and my legs turned to rubber. It was a good thing we had slowed to almost a stop. His lips brushed my ear as he whispered, "I can't wait until later."

I whispered back to him, "Me neither. Why are we whispering? They're twenty feet ahead and the wind is blowing in our faces."

"It was sexier that way." He laughed.

Judging by the size of my goose bumps, I had to agree. "They're getting away from us." I pointed ahead to Dani and Tristan who were now walking hand in hand. We quickened our steps and once again were about fifty feet behind them. They were laughing about something, and the attraction between them was palpable. I felt Erik tense beside me. *Protective daddy.* I squeezed his hand and walked even faster to catch up to the teenagers.

"Hey! Dani!" I yelled against the wind.

Erik circled his fingers, put them to his lips, and blew a perfect whistle. Dani's head whipped around, and she smiled when she saw us behind them. I was glad to see that and not disappointment on her face.

"Hey! Are you guys done with dinner already? Sara, aren't you cold? Do you want to get ice cream?" Dani fired questions at us.

"Yes. Yes. No." I laughed. "I'm too cold for ice cream at the moment, but I have gelato in the freezer at home. Can I interest you in that?"

Dani looked up at Tristan who quickly nodded a yes. "Yay!" she cried, sounding more like a five-year-old than an almost seventeen-year-old. "What flavor do you have?"

"Flavor? As in only one flavor?" I laughed. "Kiddo, you should know me better than that. I have three: salted caramel, vanilla bean, and coffee. I call dibs on the coffee."

We were almost to the boards leading up to my front door, when Drea came walking toward us, still dressed in her perfect sundress and heels. *Who wears heels at the shore?* Yes, I was totally judging her ability to choose proper footwear. I curled my lips at her, staying true to the adage, "Keep your friends close and your enemies closer."

Drea smiled in return and I heard Erik breathe out a soft curse, and that made me feel better.

When am I going to stop feeling threatened by other women?

Erik obviously had no interest in her other than helping guide her into recovery. He loved me.

So, relax yourself already.

"Hi everyone," Drea said. "Erik, I just wanted to thank you again for this evening." She reached her hand out and touched his arm. Luckily, she touched the arm that wasn't around my shoulders because I would have bitten her. "It means so much to me to have your help at this time in my life." There was a little tear in the corner of her eye and I wondered just how sincere she was. "I got so many phone numbers tonight from the other women, but I since I have this connection with you, I was hoping to get your number also. You know, in case I need to reach out for help. I'd feel better talking to someone I know."

I watched Erik's face as he digested her words. "Drea, absolutely. Reach out if you need to, but it's important to develop a strong network of women in the program. Like I told you earlier, just listen to what the other women are sharing and when you hear one that resonates with you, talk to her after the meeting." He pulled out his phone, typed in Drea's information, and sent her a text so she would have his.

Her phone dinged with Erik's text and her green eyes sparkled as she glanced down at me. "Got it," she said. "Thank you." And then her glance returned to me. "I hope you're okay with this, Sara." Her words had a hard edge that matched her eyes.

"Drea, why wouldn't I be?" I responded. "Erik is his own person and doesn't need my approval." Dani and Tristan had drifted away from us and into the Pendleton, leaving the three of us alone. I decided I'd much rather join them and started to walk away, slipping out from under Erik's arm, which had returned to my shoulders as I spoke. "I'm going inside with the kids. I'll let you two finish up here."

Drea's chin raised slightly and a frosty smile crossed her lips. I raised my chin higher and met hers with one of my own.

I sent a small prayer to the universe that there were no remnants of crab in my teeth.

"Have a good night," I said and turned back toward the house.

"Hang on, Sara. I'm coming in with you," Erik said. I watched him nod goodbye to Drea and he grabbed my hand. I gave his hand a little squeeze as I intertwined my fingers with his and we strolled up the walkway together.

I was expecting him to open the porch door for me as he always did, but he paused and pulled me close to him.

"Sara," he said, "I hate to be a broken record, but you really don't have anything to worry about with me and Drea."

I looked down at my feet and chewed my lip for a moment before looking up into his eyes. *Oh, those eyes.* His face had an earnest, worried, brow-wrinkling look.

"I know, babe. I do know that. But that woman... she's got some *really* bad, *really* jagged energy attached to her. I don't trust her, and I can't help that right now. She hasn't given me a reason to trust her and has given me a few reasons not to. So until that changes, I'm watching her closely when she's in my presence."

Of course, inside my head I was installing surveillance cameras and microphones covering a two-block perimeter, but we'll talk about that later.

We spent the rest of the evening sharing the three containers of gelato, each with their own spoon. At 9:30 p.m., Tristan stood and stretched, wished us a good night, and thanked us for the gelato. Dani followed him outside to say a more private goodbye and I watched as Erik tensed a bit, then moved so he could see outside better. Of course I joined him.

The kids smiled at each other and Tristan bent his head to place a chaste kiss on Dani's mouth. Once he walked down the boards, she returned to the living room where Erik and I were scrambling to look like we hadn't been spying on them. We failed.

"Guys!" She laughed. "C'mon. Did you think I'd do anything with you guys watching?"

Erik puffed up and tried to act like he wasn't guilty of that very act. "Just making sure my most precious little girl was in good hands," he said with a defensive tone.

Dani got up on her tiptoes and kissed her father's cheek. "I know, Dad. But I'm not a little girl anymore. I'm almost seventeen!"

A small groan escaped his throat. "I am well aware of how old you are, kiddo." He paused and continued, "We don't know this boy from Adam. I need to make sure you're safe."

I glanced over at Dani expecting to see the obligatory eye roll. I was surprised to see her crumple into her father's arms and cry softly. Erik held her tightly and made soft, cooing sounds into her hair.

My eyes filled with tears at the sight and I went into the kitchen to give them some time together. Their relationship had grown so much stronger in just a week and that made me ridiculously happy. I knew Dani and Erik had started from a place of awkwardness and unfamiliarity that can happen when people don't see each other often. I had no doubt this summer would be priceless for them both.

Tank came padding into the kitchen, probably wondering if I might feed him something, and Molly followed closely behind. After I gave them both a biscuit, they retreated to the living room crunching happily. I drank a glass of water and scrolled through my phone a bit until I felt they had enough time to have their "moment."

I found Dani and Erik sitting on the couch, heads leaning in together as if they were having a mind meld. Maybe they were. Dani looked up when she heard me enter the room. Her eyes were soft and damp and she was hiccupping a bit as if she'd had a hard cry. I saw the dampened fabric of Erik's shirt and knew she'd sobbed her heart out. Dani smiled and Erik smiled and then I smiled, and we all sniffled a bit.

"You two okay?" I asked.

"Yeah," Dani said in a shaky voice.

"Better than okay," Erik said. He had his arm around Dani's shoulders, and he squeezed her tightly. "We just needed some time to get to know each other again. I need to learn to be a dad. I'm loving every minute of this and I promise to never take it for granted." He paused for a moment. "The past week has changed my life. Changed me." He dragged his fingers through his unruly curls and shook his head. "I don't know what kind of magic you've got, Sara, but I think it's touched each one of us."

"Abracadabra," I whispered.

CHAPTER 11

Saturday dawned cloudy, with a warm west wind that promised black flies on the beach. People learned to watch the flag at the lifeguard station closely, because if that flag was showing a breeze from the bay, you did not want to venture down to the ocean. You saw a lot of waving arms, slapping hands, and packing up when that wind shifted west. My hands flapped enough in normal life—I didn't need to add black flies.

It was muggy already at 7:00 a.m. when my eyes opened, and I kicked off the covers that were making me sweat. Molly opened the eye not hidden by the blanket and watched me as I sat up and stretched. I closed the windows I'd opened the night before to take advantage of the cool evening. *Back to AC.* Molly didn't seem interested in a walk. In fact, she had resumed snoring in the time it took me to close the windows. I did my thing in the bathroom and pulled on a pair of cutoffs and a bikini top. Drying my hair upside down—more body, you know—I checked out my toes and decided it was time for a touch-up on the nail polish. Right about that time, Molly snuck up behind me and goosed me with her nose, bringing the blow drying to a quick stop. Opting for a messy bun instead, I twisted my long, still damp hair into a knot and pulled a hair tie around it.

Molly and I went downstairs, where it felt even muggier. I closed those windows and clicked on the air conditioning. We set out on our morning walk and I turned left this time, passing Erik's dark house. I could hear his air conditioning humming already. The air was thick, and Molly and I walked at a slower pace than normal. Past the dune, the opening to the beach offered a view of a dark ocean, seeming to move even slower than we were. The first black fly got me on the back of the knee and I cursed and hurried Molly along.

"Let's go!" I tugged at the leash, pulling her away from whatever she had her nose buried in. She gave me a wounded look like she had no intention of rolling in it.

By the time we got back to the house, sweat was pouring from all kinds of places and I knew another shower was going to happen. I looked up at the leaden sky and over at Erik's, which was still dark. I pictured him asleep in his bed, all tousled and soft, lips parted, no worry line between his eyes. For a moment, I let the fantasy unroll in my head. Sneaking into his house, silently climbing into his bed and placing kisses on all the places I just mentioned, plus some.

And there I was, standing in the middle of the boardwalk, smiling like a fool. And sweating. I took myself and my dog and went back in the house, where the air conditioner had done its job. The chilly air hit my damp skin and goose bumps rose all over my body. I peeled off my damp clothes and let a hot shower rinse away all the yucks. Changing once again, this time I chose a long, soft T-shirt dress that hugged the right places yet still let the important parts breathe.

Not knowing what the day held for Erik and Dani, I decided to enjoy some coffee and cereal in the living room and watch TV. After feeding Molly, I emailed the Cell and caught up with my girls, then flipped through the guide. Saturday morning TV wasn't offering much, but I danced in my seat when I saw a full day's worth of 1950s sci-fi movies in the lineup. You know the kind: radiation makes a bug or a woman or an animal fifty times its normal size and it rampages or slithers and the good guys win in the end (or do they? *insert threatening music*). They were my favorite and I settled in to munch my cereal, drink my coffee, and cheer for the giant grasshopper.

Molly woke from her nap around 10:00 a.m. and came to find me. I was knee-deep in giant ants at that point and couldn't believe how much time had passed. I looked out the window, where the sky was still a gunmetal gray and some black clouds were forming to the west. A low rumble of thunder in the distance produced a little dance out of Molly and I quickly got to my feet to get her outside before the storm hit. After slipping my feet into flip-flops and snapping on the leash, we hit the boards for a quick bathroom break. Turning left, I observed a light on in Erik's kitchen and decided to stop in for some coffee or kisses or whatever might come up. Molly handled what needed to be handled and we walked up Erik's front path. The front door was open, and I could see through the screen door that Erik, who was in the kitchen at the sink, was just as tousled as I had fantasized earlier.

I opened the screen door, called out, "Good morning," and dropped Molly's leash so she could run to the kitchen to wish Erik her own special good morning. That's the moment Drea came into view, stepping into Molly's direct path toward Erik. My dog didn't have time to redirect and slammed against Drea, knocking her backward, directly into Erik, who caught her by her boobs. You read that right.

My brain tried to process the scene, but there were so many elements and so little time. Molly thought the whole thing was a game and was jumping around the kitchen. Erik was frozen in place with a most unusual look on his face. His hands flew off Drea's breasts, which left Drea no place to go but down. And of course, Molly figured that was part of this awesome game. Drea gave a small *ooomph* as she sat rather unladylike on the floor, legs akimbo. Molly nosed her face, now within reach, and somehow a false eyelash ended up on the end of my dog's nose.

My eyes jumped from Drea, sitting on the floor with one bald eye and looking like an odd, angry cat, to Molly, happy as a clam, to Erik who, with the exception of his hands, hadn't moved a muscle and still had that funny look on his face. I was the first to move and bent down to Drea's level.

"You okay, Drea?" I asked, trying to drum up real concern. I knew she wasn't injured and was probably gloating over the fact that Erik, no matter how inadvertently, had felt her up.

Her ice-cold green glare settled on my calm gaze.

"If your dog hurt me in any way, you will pay for it," she spit, checking herself over carefully for rips, stains, and bruises.

Switching her gaze up to Erik's still stricken face, she slowly smoothed her hands over her T-shirt-covered chest and reached up a hand for help standing. "And you," she purred, "you're my hero and you already got your reward." She ran her finger down Erik's arm. "Thanks for catching me. You're always there for me, Erik. You're like my rock."

Gagging a bit, I tried to cover it with a cough, but it was an obvious gag. "Drea, I'm sorry. Molly always runs at Erik and you walked into the wrong place at the wrong time. I hope you weren't hurt."

Drea turned her sharp eyes to me. She straightened her shoulders and thrust out her double Ds. Although her face was chiseled and her lips were pursed, the non-eyelashed eye made her look like one of those before-and-after photos when they merge two photos together half and half. I stifled a giggle when it dawned on me that she had no clue how odd she looked.

I had options here. I could wait to see if she noticed her errant lashes on Molly's nose. I could be a stand-up gal and point it out. I could watch her walk eyelash-less out the door and not give a crap. I sighed internally, and perhaps a bit externally, because I knew I'd do the right thing. Although I could guarantee she'd let me walk around like that all day if the roles were reversed.

The nagging thought that had been pinging my brain since the moment Molly hit Drea finally took over and I wondered what the heck she was doing in Erik's house at this hour of the morning and how the heck did I miss her walking by? I silently cursed the giant ants. I also wondered why Erik was still strangely silent.

Molly went over to Drea and sat down in front of her.

Drea's face turned from disdain to horror when she recognized the furry addition to Molly's nose. She made a funny *pffft* sound and snatched the false eyelash from its perch. Pushing past me, she turned her head back toward Erik.

"Thanks again, Rock. I think that's what I might call you from now on… Rock." She gave a little cat smile, then seemed to remember she was holding half her makeup in her hand and opened the screen door to leave. "I'll text you later to coordinate tomorrow," she added and sashayed down the walkway.

I stood in the kitchen for a moment, chewing my lip, deciding how to handle this. Drea was here. In his kitchen at 10:00 a.m. after just talking to him the night before. I hadn't even heard from him this morning, and yet here she was. Strands of jealousy started weaving their way through my body. When I added in the view of Erik's strong, hands gripping her boobs, the anger began to rise.

"So, do we talk about your death grip on her boobs first, or the fact that she was here once again looking for your support? Support of her double Ds is more like it." My words were spoken with a sharpness that Erik hadn't heard before.

"Sara. Please. Please, can we not do this again?" He ripped his fingers through his perfectly tousled hair making it even more perfectly tousled. "The boob thing was obviously just me trying to keep her from falling. And you have to admit it was pretty damn funny. I was afraid for a second that if I grabbed too hard, I'd burst an implant." He let out a small chuckle. "I wish the humor over me getting to first base with another woman in front of my girlfriend would outweigh your obvious anger at Drea being here."

"I'm not laughing right now, Erik. I'm getting really weird

vibes from all this and you don't seem to be as concerned about what she's trying to do as I am." I looked down at my feet, my overdue pedicure forgotten. "You keep telling me you have this under control. I want to believe you. But if I keep finding her on your property when I'm not around, I'm going to kick some ass." I puffed up my own ample chest and jutted my chin. Apparently, I'm not as intimidating as I think I am, because my threat elicited a low chuckle from Erik's throat.

"Sara." Gently he placed his hands on either side of my face. "Listen to me. Look at me. Stop looking at your toes." My eyes met his. "Drea showed up here a few minutes ago. I did not invite her over and did not know she was coming. She said she had a few questions and had run out of coffee, so she came over here to get answers and caffeine. She was only here for about two minutes before you walked in. There is nothing Drea could do that would tempt me to do anything that would hurt you or our relationship." He paused for a moment and took a breath. "Sara, you have to trust me. Drea will lose interest as soon as she realizes I'm not biting her lure."

With that, he let out a big sigh and leaned against the kitchen counter. "Please?"

I leaned against him, my head tucked into his chest. His heart beat steady and strong. He smelled heavenly, like soap and coffee, and for a minute I stayed where I was, his arms around me like a safe haven. Tears stung my eyes and I nestled into him. "I promise to do my best. This is all about me and my reactions. But you have to give me some room to feel what I'm feeling. I've never been in this position before and this is all so new." I sniffled.

Erik tightened his arms around me and kissed the top of

my head. "It's new for me, too. Look, I've been single for a long time. There have been a few short relationships over the past dozen years. But I've never, ever felt like this before. And I'm not willing to chance losing this for anything."

I raised my head off Erik's chest and looked up at him. My eyes were wet, and my nose was running, but at that moment I felt safe and loved. "I know we need to sit down and talk more about our histories. We haven't even scratched the surface, and at our age we have baggage."

He chuckled. "You're right. Some bags are heavier than others. But together, no bag is too heavy."

I hadn't talked to Erik in any detail about Ron and what happened to our marriage. And I knew more from Dani about Erik and Cynthia's union than from Erik himself. That conversation needed to happen sooner rather than later. "Okay." I sniffed. "Just hold me for a second. It's still early, I'm horribly low-caffeinated and, by the way, I'm horny."

"Oh my God." Dani made loud gagging noises from the doorway to the kitchen. "Can't you old people contain yourselves?"

"Oh my God," Erik retorted. "Can't you young people respect old people's privacy?"

"Oh my God," I butted in. "Can't you both please stop calling me *old*?"

That's the moment Tank sauntered into the kitchen, looked at each of us, and continued to his food bowl. I felt completely judged by the dog now loudly chewing his kibble.

"Was that Drea teetering down the boardwalk a couple of minutes ago?" Dani asked. "Was she here?"

I chuckled at the teetering part. "Yeah, and what's with her footwear? Who in their right mind wears spike-heeled sandals on a boardwalk?"

"What did she want?" Dani paused. "She gives me a weird feeling."

I mentally high-fived Dani on picking up on Drea's jagged edges. That ability would help her out more than once during her life.

"More information from your dad. And coffee," I said with a slight edge to my voice. "And who knows what else." I couldn't help my inner bitch sneaking out occasionally. Although, if fed coffee, she usually backed off. I grabbed a mug from the holder next to the sink and poured myself a mug. Turning around, I asked father and daughter if I could pour any for them. At their affirmatives, I poured another two mugs and left them on the counter for cream and sugar options.

"I'm glad you're both here. I wanted to go over the details for tomorrow's celebration meeting," Erik said. "It starts at nine a.m., but it's right here in Lavallette and about a five-minute walk. I'd like to start walking at eight thirty so we can find good seats with my sponsee and his family."

"If Drea is walking with us, we'd better leave a lot earlier than that," I said, thinking of her usual footwear choices. Dani snorted at that one. I threw her a wink. "And that's not my inner bitch talking." *Yes, it is, Sara,* my inner bitch said. "If she's got heels on, it's going to be a slow-go to the church."

"You make a good point," Erik mused, sipping his coffee. "I'll tell her eight twenty."

The day passed uneventfully. It stayed overcast and muggy and an occasional rumble of thunder came from over the ocean. Dani spent the day with Tristan doing jigsaw puzzles in my living room. I hung out with Erik watching more sci-fi B movies and munching on junk food. The subject of Drea didn't come up again. But the subject of dinner did, and Tristan suggested ordering Chinese.

"I'll go pick it up," he offered. "Dani can help carry bags. Do you think we could include Rachel? She's alone if I eat with you guys. My mom went back to the shop."

"Of course," I said, glad takeout was offered since cooking was the last thing on my mind at the moment. "Why don't you text her and get her order, and we'll call it in around five o'clock?" I looked at my phone to see the time. "It's four thirty now."

"Cool. Thanks." Tristan sent a quick message to Rachel and his phone chirped back almost immediately. He grinned as he read it. "She's in. What time do you want her here?"

At my response of "Any time before five thirty," his fingers flew again over his phone.

"She'll be over in a few minutes. She's finishing up a little work."

Ten minutes later, Rachel knocked at the porch door and we all yelled, "Come in!" in unison.

She was smiling as she entered the living room. "Thank you so much for inviting me! I love Chinese food and I hate eating alone."

I gave her a quick hug and was struck by her physical strength. "I know this sounds cliché, but do you work out?" She was dressed in a green tank top and khaki cargo shorts, which accentuated her slim waist and well-toned arms and legs.

Rachel laughed. Her teeth were perfect, straight, and white and I made a mental note to ramp up my flossing routine.

"Nope. Believe it or not, it's from fishing. It's my passion, next to Lisa, of course." She chuckled. "I love to fish, all kinds, all ways. That's the reason we're right on the beach, so I can surf fish to my heart's content, or take a quick walk over to the bay and drop a line off the pier. You can get quite a workout fighting to bring in a big fish."

My only experience with fishing was in the early years with Ron. He also loved to fish, although not with the exuberance of Rachel. I made him put the bait on the hook and for the next couple of hours I baked in the sun, got eaten by mosquitoes, and never caught a fish. Although I snagged the line enough times that I became an expert in retying hooks. That was the one and only time fishing entered my world.

"I was itching to get out today, but the west wind and thunder nixed that," she continued. "Those black flies are murder."

"I'm itching, too," I said, absently scratching my black fly bite from earlier. "From those horrible little boogers."

After Erik called in the order, we sat and chatted until it was time for Tristan and Dani to pick it up. I tossed the keys to the Bug to Tristan and they set off for the restaurant. That was one of the best things about where we were located: so many excellent restaurants within walking distance or a short car ride.

The three of us settled in the living room and Erik perused the small CD library that came with the house.

"Not liking these choices. Is the TV Bluetooth?" he asked.

The blank stare offered him in return gave him his answer. "Never mind. I'm going to run next door for a sec and grab some good music. Be right back."

Rachel and I smiled at each other. "How long have you and Erik been together?" she asked.

"Not long. It's brand new." I grinned and blushed for some unknown reason. "Actually fell in love with his daughter before I met him. And then it was a series of mishaps and awkward situations before we actually got to know each other." There was that blush again. "I can tend to be a bit clumsy."

Rachel laughed. "Lisa is a bit clumsy too. But she's an amazing artist. If I get a break from work , I'd love to come watch you guys create. She makes magic with leather."

"Absolutely," I said. "Join us if you can! Do you work on leather too?"

"Lisa has shown me how to do a few things, but I'd rather fish or read a book to be quite honest. It's her thing and I love her passion for it." Rachel smiled as she said that. It was clear to see how much she loved her.

I heard the porch door open and once again, Tank made his entrance before Erik. The former padded over to Molly and grunted, the latter came through the doorway juggling a dozen slippery CDs.

Erik slipped the CDs into the player and hit Shuffle. A second later the sound of soft jazz filled the air. He extended his right hand down to me and I grabbed it and stood. He kissed me a soft hello and said, "This is going to be a good mix. I think you ladies will enjoy it."

Dani and Tristan came in shortly after and we dished out our dinners and settled back into our spots in the living room.

For a few minutes, the only sounds were the strains of jazz and our chewing. Both dogs were in attendance, alert for accidental droppage and the kindness of their humans. Our conversation, once restarted, revolved around the dogs, fishing, weather, and the plans for the next day.

Somewhere around 8:00 p.m. Rachel stood up to leave. "It's past my bedtime," she said with a wave. "I plan on being on the beach fishing before daybreak. Thanks again for including me. I think this is going to be a very fun summer!"

"I'll be home soon. I want to walk Tank with Dani," Tristan said. He and Dani exchanged a glance and I watched the stars form in her beautiful eyes. *Oh, please don't let him break her heart,* I begged the Goddesses.

Rachel left, and Tristan and Dani followed shortly behind with Tank and Molly. Erik and I stood at the doorway, watching the two young people stroll down the boardwalk hand in hand, pausing every few moments so the dogs could quench their smell cravings.

"Want some more coffee?" I yawned the words more than spoke them, prompting Erik to chuckle and pull me into a hug.

"Go get some sleep. It's been a long day." He stroked the side of my face softly, his fingers trailing down my neck. Chuckling at my subsequent goose bumps, he added, "And tomorrow should prove interesting. Want to meet me for coffee on my deck earlier than eight twenty? Say, seven forty-five? Drea won't be here until eight twenty and Dani will push it right up until the last minute possible."

"Sounds like a good plan." I stifled another yawn. "Are you supplying the coffee, or am I bringing coffee for two?"

"It's on me, baby. It's on me, just the way you like it." He purred those words like a kitten. The goose bumps rose again.

"The nights are too long and lonely without you." I believe there was an actual pout on my face as I spoke the words. "Stay with me a little while? Tuck me in? Soothe my back? Rub my hiney?"

Erik's arms tightened around me. "If I stay, I'm not going to stop at your hiney." His mouth got that wolflike quality again. "Maybe I will stop there or, maybe that's all I'll concentrate on."

Well, that woke the inner badass goddess up.

"So? Still want me to stay?" he asked, and yes, the smile was still on his gorgeous face.

"Yes," I whispered. "But you need to know one thing before you stay."

"What's that, baby?" he asked, with slight concern in his voice.

My voice dropped very low and got very soft. "It's an output. Not an input." My eyes dropped as low as my voice and I waited for his response.

His response came out as choked laughter and he finally sputtered, "My God, Sara, you make me laugh. I think that's one of the things I love best about you."

Grabbing his butt firmly, I whispered, "One of the things I love best about you, right here."

Stifled laughter from the porch door brought our attention to the two teenagers and two dogs staring in at us.

"Maybe it's you guys that need the chaperone." Dani laughed. "Can't leave you alone for five minutes."

"Maybe it's past your bedtime, little girl," Erik teased in

return. "But in all seriousness, don't forget we have an early morning ahead of us. I don't want to hear whining and grumbling first thing."

Maybe we shouldn't include Drea then. I'm pretty sure that was said only in my brain. I glanced at the others and didn't see anyone looking back at me, so I felt pretty confident.

Dani rolled her eyes at her father, but did so with a smile and said she was heading home with Tank, and Tristan was heading to his own house with plans of an early fishing morning with Rachel.

"I'll be home in a bit. Don't wait up," Erik said.

CHAPTER 12

My alarm clock buzzed at 6:00 a.m. I'm not one of those people who can hit a snooze alarm. It's all or nothing. Just like getting into a pool. I don't dip my toes and venture in. Just dive in. Get it over with instead of a long, dragged-out, cold, nipply process. I opened my eyes and silenced the buzz. It was still dark and Molly was already back to sleep after the alarm. Stretching languidly, my thoughts slipped around the memories of the night before, after everyone except Erik had gone. I let out a soft moan of pleasure thinking about the hours before Erik also took his leave. *That man is magic.* But this was not the time to lounge in bed thinking. This was the time to shower, do my hair, do my makeup, and choose the best possible outfit. I peeked out my bedroom window and saw the lights go on in Drea's bedroom. *Takes her a long time to look that good* was my first thought. My second thought was more of a moment of shame when I realized my alarm went off at the same time for the same reason.

After showering and liberally applying a lightly scented lotion to my tanned skin, I put on my robe and started scrunching my long hair absentmindedly while standing in front of my closet. Definitely feeling a sundress, and the forecast for the day promised to be warm and clear. I chose a long, clingy T-shirt dress, with vertical stripes in blues and greens that made my eyes pop. The dress was ankle length and went perfectly with my lace-up boho beaded sandals. A little mascara and lip gloss would complete the look, but before putting on the dress, I tossed on a beachy cover-up to walk Molly. No sense giving Drea a heads-up.

Molly followed me downstairs, and after I clipped on her leash, slipped on flip-flops, and grabbed my sunglasses, we set out for her morning constitutional. The sun was rising nicely, promising a magnificent day. We made a right at the boardwalk and walked past Drea's house, her bedroom still lit but otherwise dark. When we approached Lisa and Rachel's, I peeked through the beach entrance and saw Rachel and Tristan already near the surf, their chairs and poles set up. I whistled loudly to catch their attention, but the breeze coming off the ocean blew the whistle right back at me. We continued our stroll until Molly was ready to go back home and eat kibble, and I was ready to doll myself up and have coffee with Erik.

The early saltwater breezes off the ocean had transformed my scrunched hair into beachy waves. I sent a silent thank-you to the hair goddess for not leaving me with frizz and fuzz and stepped into my soft dress. Approving my reflection in the mirror, I sat down on my bed to slip into my gladiator-style sandals. And that's when I realized I'd never touched up the pedicure that was so sorely needed. A quick swipe with an acetone-soaked cotton ball took away the remnants of hot pink polish and left my toes looking naked, but there was no time to paint toenails. I grabbed a pair of silver hoop earrings and built an arm party out of bracelets. My tan made all the blues and greens in the jewelry and dress stand out. Sucking in my stomach a bit, I stuck out my chest and struck a pose. "Let's do this!" I said to no one since Molly stayed downstairs during my preparations.

I grabbed my cell phone and looked at the time: 7:40 a.m. Perfect timing, awesome outfit, good hair. Hearing noises from next door, I peeked out the window and saw Erik carrying out a small tray with two mugs and a pile of pastries. My stomach growled and I wasted no time scooping up my purse and sunglasses and beat feet to my guy.

Erik watched me come out of the porch and down the stairs. His eyes traveled up and down my body and he let out a low wolf whistle.

"Sara," he growled and opened his arms wide.

I closed the distance between us without tripping, although my right gladiator sandal gave up on being a gladiator and the wrapped straps slid down to my ankle in a spaghetti bundle. Silently cursing my skinny calves, I stepped out of the sandal and into Erik's waiting arms.

"I could eat you up for breakfast. That dress hugs you in all the right places," he whispered. "I can't wait to slide you out of it later."

Of course, that made me shiver, which made Erik even happier. I pulled out a chair and plopped down, ruefully sticking my unsandaled foot out. "My sandals won't stay up."

"Tie them tighter?"

"I've tried that. My feet fell asleep."

Erik chuckled. "You have the strangest problems." He turned and walked around to the side of the house where the scaffolding was. "Here." He tossed a roll of duct tape in my direction. "Try this."

The duct tape landed at my feet. "It's not zebra stripe or hot pink, so no thanks." I gave him a smirk and retied the sandal around my lower leg.

We sat in companionable silence for a few minutes, sipping our coffee and munching on pastries and enjoying the early warm breeze. The sounds of seagulls and the crashing of waves added to what was turning out to be a most amazing day. I closed my eyes and breathed it all in. Gratitude filled my heart until I thought it was going to burst, but it didn't burst. It simply overflowed into my entire body. Tears pricked my closed eyelids. Opening my eyes, Erik's face came into focus through the tears and the smile was gone. It was replaced with a look so intense and filled with love that any question I had about the way he felt about me vanished.

"I love you." My words were spoken so softly I wasn't sure he heard, but he did. His eyes looked suspiciously damp themselves.

"I love you, too, Sara, and can't imagine a more perfect way to start my day." He paused for a moment. "Unless it was opening my eyes for the first time in the morning and seeing you next to me."

Don't cry. Don't cry. Mascara will run. Nose will run. Things will drip.

I clenched my butt cheeks and forced back the tears that

threatened to undo all my perfect preparations. *Change the subject, Sara. But make sure you revisit that thought later.*

"Is Dani awake yet?" I asked, checking the time on my phone. "It's eight, and that doesn't give her much time before we have to leave."

"I heard her stirring around while I was setting up the coffee. I'm surprised she's not out here yet."

As if on cue, Dani appeared at the front door and joined us on the deck. She looked adorable in white shorts and purple tank top. Her long hair was swept up in a ponytail, and a little mascara highlighted her long lashes.

"Good morning!" she chirped.

Erik and I exchanged a glance. Dani wasn't usually out of bed until well after nine and never in this good of a mood.

"Good morning, yourself. To what do we owe the blessing of such a good mood so early in the day?" Erik asked.

Dani simply wrinkled her nose at him and said, "Oh, Daddy, you're so silly." She picked up a pastry and nibbled the edge.

"Silly? I'm *silly?*" Erik laughed at his daughter. He looked over at me. "She hasn't called me daddy since she was ten."

"I'm going to run down to the beach to see Tristan before the meeting, okay? I promise to be back before eight twenty." Dani held her cell phone up to show she'd watch the time. "Can I bring them each a pastry?" Without waiting for an answer, she scooped up two of the tasty delights and wrapped them in a napkin. "See you in a few minutes!" she called out as she trotted down the boardwalk.

"Tristan." Erik shook his head. "There you have it. But I'm not complaining. Not one bit. As long as she's safe and he treats her well, I'll be happy to enjoy all the good moods she's willing to offer." He paused and sniffed. "And I'll take all the 'daddys' I can get, too."

"Exactly." I covered his hand with mine. "I have a good feeling about Tristan. He's a great kid, and I think Dani really likes him."

Erik watched Dani skipping down the boards, pastries gripped in each hand, until she reached the opening to the beach and disappeared.

"Yeah, I know. I love seeing her happy." He said it in a low voice, and in an even lower voice continued, "I love seeing you happy too. Last night was fun. All of it."

My skin rose in goose bumps, but not at Erik's words. They rose in response to a familiar click. The *tap-tap* of inappropriate beach footwear on a boardwalk. *Stop judging, Sara.* I looked toward Drea's house and sure enough, there she was. Clickety-clacking down the boards toward us looking like a million dollars. A white halter top, exposing plenty of tata, and a wrap-around peasant skirt in the exact same ice-green color as her eyes. Spike-heeled strappy sandals completed the outfit.

We watched in silence as Drea expertly maneuvered down the boardwalk, each heel coming down perfectly on a board and not a crack. *How did she learn to do that so quickly?* My inner bitch wanted to critique everything about her. But my inner bitch was smart enough to realize I'd also taken great care with my outfit for the morning. However, *my* tatas weren't on full view.

"She bends over the wrong way and one of those puppies is going to pop out," I muttered.

"There will probably be more than a few guys there who

wouldn't consider that the 'wrong way,'" Erik said with a chuckle. "But I'm not one of them. I promise, one of those gets loose and my eyes will not leave yours."

Drea reached Erik's front deck and gave us one of her icy looks. "Good morning." She eyeballed the coffee and Erik quickly offered her a to-go cup to bring along on the walk. After gratefully accepting, we stood to leave. As I took my first step, the gladiator straps tied around my left calf let loose. Sighing, I stared down at my ankle and distinctly heard Drea's soft snort. Erik quickly dropped to one knee in front of me. *Don't think that didn't give my heart an extra beat or two.*

"Let me tie them. Your calves get thinner when you stand up."

"But what happens when I sit down?" I asked. "My feet are going to fall asleep again."

Drea snorted again, not so subtly this time. "Maybe you should stick to flip-flops, Sara. They seem more suited to your… body type."

So many words entered my mind. I bit them back one by one, refusing to lower myself to her mean-girl level. "You know what, Drea? You may be right. I'm going to run next door and grab a pair."

Drea's shoulders sagged a bit when I didn't take her bait. "Be right back," I called as I headed to my porch, first slipping the unfortunate but adorable gladiator sandals off my feet.

Just as I got to my porch door, Dani came skipping back down the boardwalk toward home. She waved and followed me into the Pendleton. "I just have to switch sandals," I explained. "And then we're ready to roll." After slipping into my favorite blue flip-flops, we crossed the sand to Erik's. Drea hadn't wasted a moment alone with him and was sitting in the seat I'd vacated minutes earlier. When she caught sight of us heading toward them, she touched Erik's arm and threw her head back and let out a laugh.

"You're so amusing!" she said loud enough for Dani and me to hear. Erik gave her a bemused look but said nothing.

"Isn't he though?" I said softly and stood behind his chair wrapping my arms around him. "He makes me laugh all the time." I kissed the top of his head and gave him a hug.

Drea's lip twitched, but her smile didn't falter. "You're a lucky woman, Sara. I hope you know how lucky you are."

I wasn't sure if anyone else present heard the threat in her voice. It might have been just me. "Don't you worry your pretty little head, Drea. I know how lucky we both are."

Erik rose and took my hand. "Let's get walking."

We reached the meeting in record time, Drea clicking along the sidewalk without issue. The church was a huge, stone building with spires and gorgeous stained glass windows. I hadn't been inside a church in many years, save for various weddings, funerals, and the AA meetings I attended with my brother. We followed Erik down the side of the church and through a door that led down a staircase to the basement where the meeting would be held. We entered a large room, with long cafeteria tables set up in a big square, lined with chairs. Inside the square of tables sat an empty chair. My brother taught me that the empty chair represented those who were still out and suffering.

A few people were milling around, talking in small groups and gathered around the coffee pot. A large sheet cake with the words "Congratulations" printed on the icing looked delicious and my stomach growled in anticipation. Erik spotted his sponsee sitting down already with a cup of coffee in front of him. He looked to be around mid-thirties, small and trim, neatly dressed in khaki pants and a blue golf shirt. A young woman sat directly behind him in a row of chairs behind the others, with a toddler sitting on her lap. After hugging the young man and kissing the woman on the cheek, Erik tousled the child's curls and turned to introduce us.

"This is John and Debbie, and this little guy is Michael." We exchanged pleasantries and names and put our belongings down on chairs next to them. "Does anyone want coffee?" Erik asked as he headed to the urn.

I opted for a bottle of water, having had enough coffee already that my lower lip was vibrating. Knowing the row of chairs behind the main tables were for family and guests, I put the sweater I brought just in case it was cold on the chair behind Erik and right beside Debbie and Michael. Dani put her to-go cup on the chair beside me. I watched Drea's face as she realized the seat next to Erik was open. Moving as quick as a weasel, she put her cup on the table next to his. Turning slowly, she met my eyes and fake smiled. "Do you want me to explain to you how the meeting is run?" she asked fake sweetly.

"No, but thanks," I responded in a neutral tone, trying to keep the rising anger out of my voice. "My brother is in program and I've attended a number of celebration meetings with him. So don't you worry about us. We're fine back here." I put my arm around Dani and fake smiled right back at her.

Dani muffled a chuckle and rose to play with baby Michael, who was starting to fuss in his mother's lap. Debbie gave Dani a grateful look and handed the squirming boy over. She brought Michael to the corner of the room, where a small play area was available for the kids to keep occupied. Within moments, they were both sitting on colorful mats and playing with building blocks.

"How old is he?" I asked Debbie.

"Fifteen months. He's all boy, never stops moving, touching, crawling, and getting into mischief," she said, her lips turning up.

I noticed the dark circles under her eyes and imagined her downtime was limited. "He's adorable. And look how happy he is with Dani!" We watched to two play for a moment, and then my eyes searched the room.

More people had arrived while we were chatting. Many grabbed coffees and sat down without talking to anyone.. I spotted Erik surrounded by five women. This didn't surprise me in the least, and I wondered if any of them knew who he was in his not-so-anonymous life. They all gazed up at him like he held the secret to the holy grail. Erik was talking and laughing, seemingly oblivious to the adoration from the fangirls in front of him. I wiggled in my seat a tiny bit, knowing he was coming home with me, and only me. *Wish all you want, ladies.*

Drea's reaction to Erik's fan club was much different from mine. I watched her eyes crackle with ice. *What the hell are her eyeballs made of?* Her body was literally vibrating as much as my lower lip. *And why is she so jealous of the attention my boyfriend is getting?* Both questions stymied me. And both questions made me realize the height of Drea's attraction to Erik. I watched as she put her cup down to save her seat and walk over to Erik and his flock. *Grab the popcorn.* She slithered into the group on Erik's right, seemingly pushing the woman previously in that spot to her right. Drea and the evicted woman exchanged dirty looks, and I heard soft laughter from the corner seat at the table. An older woman, knitting something in a gorgeous shade of aqua, was trying to stifle the chuckles that kept spilling out of her mouth. Her laughter made me laugh and she turned to look at me.

"I'm sorry!" I said quickly. "But your laughter is contagious even though I don't know what you're laughing about."

"Actually, I think you do know. Hi, my name is Dottie. You're here with Erik? Are you his girlfriend? He's spoken about you in meetings. It's nice to meet you."

I responded in kind, and we exchanged generalities about the weather. Soon, Debbie chimed in about the weather we'd had the day before.

"I heard talk online about a possible storm for this week. The forecasters wouldn't say much because it's too early to predict, but they said if everything comes together it could be a pretty bad storm," Debbie said with a worried tone. "You guys are right on the beach, aren't you? We're a block down and a block over, closer to the bay."

Dottie frowned. "I hope they're wrong. They probably are. They usually are. I'm not going to even think about it yet. Bigger fish to fry in my life." With that, Dottie turned back around after one last amused look toward Drea. Over her shoulder she mouthed, *Watch her.*

Knowing Dottie could see me with her peripheral vision, I nodded slowly. *Yes, Dottie, I'm aware.*

The meeting leader, an older man with gray hair and a beard, moved to his place at the head of his table and slapped his hand down on the table. "It's time, folks. Let's take seats and get this meeting started."

All the people milling around found seats at either the table or behind their loved ones also celebrating sober anniversaries. Erik's sponsee wasn't the only person celebrating today. Typically AA meetings held a celebration event at the end of each month during regular meeting time. Anyone wanting to have an anniversary acknowledged would simply notify the meeting leader. By the looks of the crowd, and the number of people sitting with cards and gift bags in front of them, there were five people celebrating. Dani handed a sleeping Michael back to his mother and took her seat to my left.

"Hi. My name is Frank, and I'm an alcoholic," stated the meeting leader.

"Hi, Frank!" the room said in unison. After he read the opening affirmations, Frank explained to the room about the celebrations.

"We have five celebrants today, John, Pam, and Kevin with thirty days, Vicky with five years, and Oscar with forty years!"

Clapping broke out in the room as we showed our support for the five people from five different walks of life and the journey they were on.

"We start with the thirty-day celebrants and work our way to Oscar," Frank said with a proud smile on his face. Oscar was sitting next to him, the table in front of him piled high with cards and gifts. "Let's start with Pam, celebrating thirty days." Because the room was so crowded, each celebrant and their sponsor stood at their place at the table. Two women stood, one youngish, maybe twenty-five, the other a matronly woman with a friendly face. The young woman was visibly shaking, her hands twisting around each other and the napkin clutched between them.

Barb spoke first, telling us about how Pam had come into the rooms knowing at this early age that she had a problem. That Pam wanted to be here and wanted to succeed. Pulling a shiny large coin from her pocket, Barb pressed the coin into her sponsee's hand. "You've made it thirty days. I know you can do this. I'm so proud of you for the hard work you've done already."

Tears pricked my eyes and I mentally berated myself for not choosing waterproof mascara. I had a feeling there would be many eye blots and nose wipes in my future and was glad I'd squirreled away an extra napkin after the pastries were eaten.

Pam stood for a moment, staring down at the coin in her hand. In a shaky voice, she spoke a few words about her life and how grateful she was to be exactly where her feet were meant to be planted. Her tears started flowing after her first few words, and I heard Dani sniff beside me and press her own napkin against her nose.

When they were done, both women sat down, and Frank called for Kevin to be recognized. Similar stories were told, and another coin was presented.

I watched Drea lean into Erik's shoulder and whisper something in his ear. He nodded but never made eye contact. When Frank announced John's name, Erik and John rose in unison and introduced themselves to the room.

Erik looked handsome and self-assured, John's coin already in his hand.

"John, I know the last thirty days have felt like a lifetime to you. I know there were days you didn't think you could make the next twenty-four hours without a drink. But you did it, buddy, you did it. You are working a strong program and if you keep on this track, someday we'll be standing up here celebrating your forty years." Erik pressed the coin into John's hand and shook his other. "I'm proud of you. One day at a time."

Debbie's shoulders shook and when I turned to her, tears flowed freely down her cheeks. Her arms held her sleeping child, and her tears soaked his soft curls. I put my arm around her and left it there while John spoke.

"Hi again, John, alcoholic."

"Hi, John."

"I don't really know what to say. I tried so many times to stop. I've never made thirty days before." John looked around the room. "I promise to keep this short. You guys probably want cake."

The room laughed at his joke and John seemed to relax a bit. "There's a couple of people I have to acknowledge. First my wife." John looked over at Debbie. "You and Michael are my world. I'm going to make it this time. I'm sorry I made your life hell. Thank you for being here with me."

Debbie smiled through her tears and blew him a kiss. John made a show of catching the kiss and putting it in his pocket, eliciting another chuckle from the room.

"And Erik. Man, you are the coolest dude I ever met. You have been there for me from day one. You make me want to be a better man."

That's when my eyes overflowed and I pressed the already

damp napkin against my eyes, trying to keep the mascara in place.

After Erik and John sat down, John turned around and touched Debbie's knee. She reached her hand out and covered his, and they held that gaze for a moment before Frank called the next celebrant's name.

The rest of the meeting was just as touching, especially when Frank gave Oscar his forty-year coin. The two men told a few hysterical stories from the early days in the program. People who think AA meetings are all doom and gloom should attend an open celebration meeting just once. There were as many laughs as there were tears.

While Oscar was speaking, a few of the members started passing out pieces from the sheet cake. We chewed our cake and sipped our coffee and enjoyed the rest of the hour.

The meeting closed with Frank leading the Serenity Prayer. I watched as members stood, grabbed their trash, and folded their chairs, bringing them to the wall where they were stacked. There was always a "meeting after the meeting," and after giving Erik a kiss and telling him how awesome he was, I pushed him to go do his thing while Dani and I played with baby Michael. Drea folded her chair and followed Erik over to the stack. Always the gentleman, he took the chair from Drea and added it to the others.

Erik's fan club quickly moved around him again, but I saw him kindly step out of their circle and make his way to Oscar for some conversation. The women's faces fell, and they joined other groups. Drea was watching Erik from the cake table. She wasn't cleaning up the cake like other people were doing, nor was she gathering forgotten Styrofoam cups. She was simply leaning against the table watching Erik.

Dottie moved to leave and paused in front of me. "You hear me child?" she asked. "Be aware. That's a predator."

"I hear you, Dottie. And I am, trust me, I am."

"Are you talking about new woman with the red hair?" Debbie asked. "She's quite beautiful, but that's one unhappy woman." She paused, rocking Michael absentmindedly on her knee. "I guess she's in the right place. But she looks at men like they're a meal. That sounds judgey, I guess. Maybe her vibe's throwing me off."

Dottie and I nodded in agreement, and she turned away to say goodbye to others. Michael started fussing again and Debbie stood, grabbed her diaper bag, and excused herself to the restroom. My eyes were drawn back to where Drea was still standing at the food table. A guy who looked to be in his forties was standing quite close to her, trying to engage her attention. Drea was looking at him through slitted eyes, a close-lipped smile on her face. The guy gave up after a minute and left her side to approach another woman.

"I'm going to go talk to Drea for a minute. Do you want to come with me?" I asked Dani. She stood and followed me to Drea's statue-like form leaning against the table. As Dani and I approached, Drea's eyes stopped searching the room and focused on us coming closer. For a brief second, her face took on the look of a dog about to puke. You know how they get that flat, squished face? She recovered quickly, replacing it with an icy glare.

"Hey, Drea. Wasn't that a great meeting?" I asked.

"I guess. I've only been to a couple of meetings, so I really don't know what to expect as far as greatness," she said coolly. "Have you seen Erik? I can't spot him anywhere and I need to talk to him."

"No, I haven't really been watching him." I took a quick glance around the room and spotted his handsome face as he talked intently with an older woman in the far corner of the room. "There he is." I pointed in his general direction and turned to face the table to see if any help was needed in cleaning up.

Apparently, I put my hand back down on the table without realizing the tie to Drea's skirt was lying there. Everything happened in a split second, yet it would remain burned in my brain forevermore. Once Drea saw Erik, she pushed herself away from the table to head toward him. She would have made it, too, had my hand not been in its unfortunate location.

As her long legs took a stride, the bow untied and the skirt slid to the floor in a move not even an experienced stripper could have pulled off. For a moment Drea froze midstride, her skirt around her ankles, her black lace thong showing off all her below-the-waist attributes. Her jaw dropped, she looked down, and then she became aware of the stares, gasps, and oh my gawds. She also became aware of the palpable sensuality of her situation, and the openly interested eyes of most of the men still in the room. I saw all this cross her face in a split second, before she slowly reacted.

"You bitch!" Drea spat in my direction. "You fucking did that on purpose." She pulled off another stripper move as she crouched down to grab the material circling her feet. On her way back up, she made sure to look directly at Erik and hold her gaze on his as she wrapped the errant skirt around her waist. But she quickly turned back to me to finish her tongue-lashing. "Admit it! You're not actually clumsy. You know exactly what you're doing, don't you?"

I'm pretty sure my jaw was still open from the initial skirt drop at this point. "Drea, first of all I would never do that on purpose. Second of all, this is not the time nor the place for this." *I'm not quite sure where my balls were coming from, but my inner goddess was cheering my ass on.*

"Bullshit!" she hissed, turned on her heel, and headed for the door.

I followed behind her, although I'm not sure why. I knew she'd brush off any attempt of mine to convince her it wasn't done on purpose.

"Sara… is she alright? I can't believe that just happened." Erik rushed up behind me as I went through the door behind Drea.

My short legs were trying to keep up with Drea's long ones, and Erik overtook me easily. The moment Drea heard Erik's voice behind her, she slowed her pace and the icy façade of her face changed to a mixture of sly and coy as she turned toward him.

"Erik, ohmygod I'm so embarrassed. How can I face any of those people again?" she whimpered.

"Drea, calm down. It's not like you were naked. It's nothing more than we would see this afternoon at the beach." Erik spoke in a measured, even voice.

Batting her eyelashes, she wiped an imaginary tear from the corner of her eye. "I guess you're right. Luckily, I didn't go commando today. I usually do."

Just when I thought the day couldn't possibly get any

crazier, Drea said something that took my breath away.

"But Erik already knew that." She giggled and pushed his shoulder jokingly. "Right, Erik?"

Erik's face remained stony. His mouth remained closed, his lips pursed. I could hear the wheels turning in his head. His eyes moved from Drea's to mine and he directed his words to me.

"Sara, I swear to you the only reason I know that is because Drea mentioned it in passing during one of our talks."

"I did have you going for a minute though, didn't I, Sara?" Drea sneered. "Consider it payback."

My brain was exploding with facts and innuendos and flashes of Drea's skirt sliding down her long legs.

I clenched my butt cheeks to avoid the tears that insisted on brimming over my lower lids. Erik opened his mouth to speak, but before he could, I choked out, "I need to just take some time for myself right now. Don't say anything. Either of you." I looked at the faces staring back at me in various states of shock, confusion, and gloating. Erik looked green, and right at that moment I didn't have enough left inside me to try to reassure him everything would be okay. Mostly because I didn't know if it was going to be okay. I needed to think and standing in a parking lot with the man I loved, and the viper who wanted him, was not conducive to being able to do that necessary thinking.

I swallowed down tears. *Do not cry. Do not cry. Speak your truth!* "I'm going to walk the beach on the way back. I'd like to do that alone so that I can figure out a few things, like why you are so hell-bent on getting in between Erik and me. Or why you can't take no for an answer." *Where are these words coming from? How on earth am I even forming sentences at this point?*

Drea stared at me, her mouth open and her eyebrows high on her porcelain-skinned forehead. I turned my attention to Erik, standing slouched over, his thumbs hooked into the pockets of his jeans. He raised his eyes to mine, and they held an imploring look.

I lifted a finger to his lips. "I need to sort through this and figure out why I'm feeling what I'm feeling. I also don't understand why you continue to let her do and say the things she does. And mostly, I just need to get away from Drea before I say or do something I might regret." I paused for a moment and shifted my glance to Drea. "And you're totally not worth it."

I turned to walk away before I could see her reaction, but I heard her sharp intake of breath. *Good. Maybe I got through to her.* But no. After that sharp intake, her soft exhale contained one word. "Bitch." I turned around to face her and she continued, "That's a good question, isn't it, Sara? Why doesn't he shut it down, I wonder."

I continued walking away. By this time, Dani had broken away from the inside crowd at the door and I waved and pointed back to where her father still stood with the ice queen. She nodded, a worried look on her face. A pang of guilt hit my heart and although I wanted to take her in my arms, that had to wait until after I'd had a good long talk with myself.

I knew my emotions were working overtime. The meeting had so many moments of grateful tears, the after-meeting fiasco with the skirt and then my outburst in the parking lot and Drea's mic drop question just now was making my brain crave solitude. I blew Dani a kiss, forced a smile, and mouthed *See you later* to her. She nodded uncertainly and walked toward her father instead of following me.

I walked as quickly as I could toward the crosswalk and the universe was with me, the *walk* light blinking on just as I approached. I kept up the brisk pace as I crossed the road and headed up the sidewalk toward the boardwalk and beach. As I approached the dune entrance, I was glad to see it was still early enough that I didn't need my beach badge. I slipped out of my flip-flops and dug my toes into the soft, already warm sand.

The beach was still empty, the fishermen just starting to pull in their lines and pack away their tackle boxes until trying again tomorrow. I zigzagged between the gentle waves of ocean in low tide, splashing my toes, and walking behind the remaining fishing poles so as not to tangle myself in their invisible lines. I noticed a good long stretch of beach in front of me with no impediments, which meant I could walk at the water's edge and not pay attention. As I walked, I let my mind wander to what had happened, Drea's words, Erik's face, my words, Drea's perfect body and long legs. I felt jealousy, anger, and disappointment toward Erik for not immediately shutting Drea out of his life. And once I felt all that, I realized how childish and controlling that sounded.

I mentally checked off all the things I knew to be absolutely true. I knew I loved Erik. I knew I strongly disliked Drea. I knew Drea was a manipulator. I knew Drea's breasts were fake. That last truth just slipped out. But it was true. Those were my truths as I knew them. I realized I barely knew Erik and to entrust him with my love and allow him into my soul, to trust him, to really trust him, that's where my truth wavered. How could I know for sure? *But how could anyone know for sure?* It would be rare to trust someone immediately without getting to know them first. Erik spoke all the right words and used all the right body language. His eyes didn't waver when he looked into my eyes and told me he loved me.

That brought another memory back to the forefront of my brain. The memory of Ron, of our marriage, of how stifled I felt. I'd married too young, and my husband became more distant and colder as the years went on. Whatever spark we'd felt in those early years had long since turned to dust. His rare proclamations of love weren't while looking deeply into my eyes and soul the way Erik's were. They were spoken randomly at the end of our phone conversations or before he left on a business trip.

Our life was a solitary union. Children never happened, and neither of us questioned the whys. It simply became part of us. It was quiet and cool, and for a long time I didn't know any better. It was my normal. I'd look at the relationships of the people around me and they weren't all love and roses either, so I accepted my normalcy but always wondered if the grass was greener. So the day I caught him in his affair with Bronwyn I felt more relief than anger or betrayal. I saw my way out to start a new life. Our divorce was quick, without much drama, and the day after the papers were signed, I was already moving into my small condo. And life moved on.

Molly became my focus and the recipient of all my love, and I grew to cherish the quiet of being alone. The quiet when you're not alone had been so awkward for so long that the ability to be my own boss, 100 percent in charge of my life and ready to experience new things, new people, new places felt so freeing. Our divorce settlement paid for my condo plus some, so when my boss decided to retire and gifted me the season at the Jersey shore, I had no strings tying me down. That brought me to where I stood today, my feet dug in the sand, sinking deeper and deeper as the waves gently crashed against my legs.

I realized I'd been standing in one spot for a long time judging by where the sun was in the sky and the fact that my legs below the knee were mostly buried in sand. Grateful Erik hadn't followed me, I pulled each leg out of the suctioning sand and started heading toward the Pendleton where I had a feeling he would be waiting. Waiting for what my reaction would be. Waiting to see if I believed he loved me. If I trusted him. My entire heart wanted to believe him. I wanted to float off into the glorious future with my amazing and gorgeous lover. I wanted to believe him.

I just didn't know for sure if I could. And I didn't know how long it would take me to get there.

Knowing Molly would be anxious to go out, I decided to walk back to the house on the boardwalk instead of the sand. My guts were rolling around almost as much as my brain, which I knew was all due to stress. It felt like that sick feeling I used to get in the back seat of my parents' car. As I drew closer to the Pendleton, I saw Drea on her porch, scrolling through her phone and looking bored. I looked past Drea, scanned my front yard, and seeing it empty continued my gaze to Erik's house. Also empty. My stomach relaxed a bit. Drea I could ignore from now until the end of time without blinking. It was Erik who knotted my stomach and the fact that he wasn't waiting for me at my porch door or his gave me a little twinge of fear.

Molly was waiting for me as I approached the door, tail wagging and with a huge golden retriever grin. I grabbed the leash, hooked her up, and turned around slowly so as not to fall off the porch steps again. I could almost hear Drea's icy laughter if that had happened. *Bitch.* I could still hear her whispered curse in my ears, and a warm flush of anger grew inside me. Better to turn left and walk the boards in the opposite direction from her. As I passed Erik's house, Dani came running out of the house.

"Sara! Wait!" she called out. "Can I walk with you? Are you okay? You looked so upset at the church and dad has been quiet and gloomy since we left the meeting."

"Of course you can walk with me," I said when she reached my side. I put my arm around her. "I'm okay. I am upset, but that's on me right now. I have a choice how I'm going to react to any situation, and as much as I want to forget this morning ever happened, I have to figure out why I react so violently toward Drea." I paused as Molly stopped to sniff a clump of seagrass. "I've never been a jealous person, and I don't know where this comes from—"

Dani interrupted me. "Sara, I don't blame you for being upset and jealous. I sure would be if someone threw themselves at my boyfriend the way Drea throws herself at Dad." She blushed a bit when she said *boyfriend*. "But please don't break up with him because of it, please?"

I looked into her eyes and saw her anxiety clearly on her

face. "Dani." I drew her in for a hug. "I love your father. I love you. I don't love my possessive jealousy, which could impact every facet of our relationship. It wants me to believe terrible things. It leads me to not trust him. And that's what I need to come to terms with. Breaking up with your dad is the last thing in the world I want right now. But I have to figure out what this stems from and get rid of it before it poisons us."

Dani's eyes filled with tears. "Please don't leave us, Sara. We need you. We both need you." Her tears spilled over and I held her tightly, loving this young woman so much.

Molly, who up until that moment and been patiently sitting by my side, started pulling me toward the Pendleton. I knew only one person caused that reaction. Erik. Sure enough, he was headed toward Dani and me with an expression that could only be described as worried with a dash of fear. I let go of the leash and Molly made a beeline for Erik and he ruffled her soft fur as she leaned against him.

"Sara?" he said softly. "Are you okay? I've been worried. You've been gone over an hour. I know we need to talk about what happened, but something has come up that I need to talk to both of you about."

"I'm okay. Thanks for being worried. I just need some time. And yes, we do need to talk about what happened this morning."

We walked back to Erik's front deck and the three of us sat down to hear Erik's news.

"I just got a message from my agent. He's been generating some prerelease media for the book I'm working on now. He's booked me a five-day media blitz starting in Manhattan, and heading to DC and Raleigh after that." He took a deep breath.

"Two things. One, I have to leave very early in the morning and I hate taking off after what happened and don't want to leave with us like this. Two, I have to ask you if you could have Dani and Tank stay with you at the Pendleton starting tonight, which, after this morning, feels like a big ask."

"No, no of course Dani and Tank can stay with me," I answered. "No worries, and maybe a few days apart is exactly what I need to think things through." I gazed at my toes, waiting for him to disagree with me. That felt a bit manipulative on my part, but my world was a little wacky at the moment to say the least.

"Maybe it is," Erik said quietly. "I have a ton of pre-trip stuff to get ready this afternoon. May I text you later to see if we can talk?"

I pressed my lips together, wrestling with wanting to jump into his arms and saying everything was fine and we were good and I love you, and wanting to save myself possible heartbreak by keeping space between us while I sorted myself out. *Don't push him away, Sara.*

"Sure," I replied, turning to Dani. "Maybe you should pack some toiletries so you don't have to constantly run back and forth for things you might need."

Dani nodded and started off toward their home, calling over her shoulder, "Can I choose which room I stay in, Sara?"

"Absolutely." I turned back to Erik. "Text me later on, okay?"

"Yeah." He bit his lip and reached out for my hand. "Sara, we're going to get this straightened out. Just know that I love you. I'll text you." With a squeeze of my hand, he turned and walked back to his house.

Molly looked up at me and I bent down to grab her leash. While I was down there, she gave me a huge kiss across my forehead, making my bangs stick straight up like Cameron Diaz in *There's Something About Mary*. Laughing, I hugged my fur-faced angel. She always knew when my heart was feeling bruised and tender. *Good dog.*

I unlocked my front door and Molly followed me inside. I looked at the carnage that I call a worktable and promised myself art time over the next week while Erik was away. *"Art heals,"* whispered one of the Goddesses in my head. "So does chocolate," I whispered back and went straight to the kitchen to have a piece.

CHAPTER 13

Dani came over at four, carrying a huge duffel bag and huffing under its weight.

"Did you bring everything you own?" I joked.

"Well, you know I figured if I was going to stay here, I might as well bring everything I might need so I don't have to go back over there until Dad comes back." She took a breath and added, "I'm going to make believe I live here. With you. To see what it's like, you know, in the future. Unless..." Her voice dropped off and her eyes held questions.

The future. I felt like everything I thought might be in my future, everything I wished and dreamed, had a blanket thrown on top. *Am I going to have a future with Erik? With Dani? With Tank?* Tears pricked my eyes and I drew Dani into a hug.

"My sweet girl. Let's not go to *unless* unless we have to." I mustered a smile. "Let's enjoy the next week together and make art and have tons of girl talk and beach time and long dog walks every day."

Dani returned my quivering smile with one of her own. "I love you, Sara. I just want you and Dad to be together and be happy. I know he loves you and I know he doesn't love Drea. I don't think he even likes her."

Truth time. "It's not so much about how your dad feels about her. It's about my reaction to her and the perceived threat. I've always said I'm not a jealous person but apparently, I *actually am* a jealous person. And that's on me, Dani, not your dad." I didn't add that I was disappointed in Erik for not shutting Drea down.

"But Drea throws herself at him all the time. I've seen it and I've heard it. Even though Dad doesn't buy into it, I don't blame you for being jealous. I'd be just the same." Dani shook her head as she spoke. "I think we should do something about it. Neutralize the enemy type stuff."

The Cell had a running joke about keeping the bail jar ready if needed. I wondered if I should shoot off a quick email.

"Are we talking bloodshed or sticking needles into a voodoo doll type stuff?" I asked trying not to laugh.

Dani's eyes got big. "I've been reading about voodoo dolls and I don't think we should do that."

"Soooo, bloodshed then?"

"No! No bloodshed." She laughed. "We have all week to come up with a plan."

Dani ran back to her house and returned with Tank and his bowls and a bag of kibble. I got him all situated in the kitchen with water and food and turned to Dani.

"So, which bedroom did you choose?" I asked.

"The attic room!" she exclaimed. The attic was one huge room with multiple beds and dormers overlooking both the bay and ocean. "I'm going to go choose which bed right now!"

She ran off to climb the stairs. "Yell down and let me know so I can pull out the correct sheets," I called up to her.

A muffled "okay" came from the second floor and I heard the doorway to the attic squeak loudly. I grabbed a can of WD-40 from the closet and put it on the stairs so I could take care of that right away. I could hear Dani moving around in the attic, deciding which bed was best. Visions of three little bears danced in my head.

"The queen please!" Dani called from two stories above me.

I called out an acknowledgment and added a clean set of queen sheets next to the WD-40. Dani came bounding down the stairs and grabbed both things off the steps, pivoted, and ran back upstairs. "Do you need help making the bed?" I called up to her.

"Nope, I'm good, but what's the WD-40 for?" she asked as she opened the door to the attic. The squeak answered her question before I could. "Never mind. Should I ask Dad to take care of it?"

By this time, I was climbing the stairs so we wouldn't have to yell back and forth. "Ask Dad? Heck no. We've got this covered. We are strong, smart, capable women."

I rounded the corner to where Dani was standing in the open attic doorway. She was holding the can as if it were a snake. I muffled a giggle. "It's not going to bite you."

She laughed. "It's oily and I don't want to get it on the sheets." Turning, she continued up the stairs after handing me the spray can. "Hold this, okay? I'll throw these on the bed and come back down to help you."

While I waited for her to come back downstairs, I opened and closed the door a few times to make sure I could pinpoint which hinge was the troublemaker. The top one seemed to be the culprit. Why the universe laughs at me so often, I'll never know. I went up two steps and stuck the little red straw in the little hole in the spray nozzle. I'd seen Ron do this dozens of times. Pressing the nozzle yielded a healthy squirt into all the hinge areas I could find. As Dani came down the stairs to help, I was already wiping up some errant WD-40 and swinging the now silent door open and closed.

"You did it, Sara!" she exclaimed, clapping her hands.

Smiling back at her, I took a bow and smacked my head on the banister. "Don't say a word. Not a word. I'm fine," I said, rubbing my forehead.

She turned and ran back up the stairs to her attic room.

"Do you need any help up there?" I called after her.

"Nope! All good here," came a choked reply from Dani, obviously trying to hide her laughter.

"It's okay," I said with a dramatic sigh and a laugh. "You can laugh with me." I turned to go back down to the first floor, and I listened to her laughter until I was halfway down the stairs.

Just before 5:00 p.m., Erik's text came in.

> **ERIK**
> Hey, can we talk?

> **SARA**
> Sure, where?

> **ERIK**
> Over here. I'm guessing Dani is busy setting herself up, so we'll be alone.

> **SARA**
> Be over in a minute.

"Dani?" I called up two flights of stairs. Nothing. I decided to make good use of modern technology and texted her that I was going next door to talk to her dad and to make herself at home until I got back.

I ran into the bathroom to see what I looked like. My hair was up in a messy bun, and I'd done nothing with myself after the long walk other than shower off the salt, sand, and tears. My tan looked very dark against my tie-dyed sundress and helped cover the puffy eyes that screamed, *YES, I cried through my shower.* Staring at my reflection in the mirror, I mentally hugged myself and straightened my crown like the warrior goddess I was.

"Let's do this," I whispered and headed out the door.

The walk next door wasn't long enough to gather my surging thoughts. I took a deep breath and knocked on Erik's front door. It swung open immediately, like he'd been tracking my moves since his text.

"Hey," he said softly. "You okay? I've been trying to get everything ready to go here, but my brain just won't shut off thinking about you and what you're thinking about us and what's going on."

Drawn to him like a moth to a flame, all I could think was

how could I not move into his arms? *Tell me you love me, Erik. Just tell me you love me and you need me and you'll close yourself off to the she-witch.*

He enveloped me in his arms, and I laid my head on his chest. I closed my eyes and willed myself to be strong, but his pounding heart filled my ear and I realized he was as afraid as I was.

"Sara, I need to know where your head is. I can't leave when things are like this, and I have to leave, so we should sit down and talk this out."

Well, those weren't the exact words I wanted to hear, but they were fine for an opener. Erik grabbed my hand and led me to the couch, where we sat and faced each other.

I took a deep breath and started talking. "So let me get my words all out before you say anything, okay? I did a lot of thinking on my walk. I'm trying to come to terms with my reaction to Drea's obvious intentions toward you, and while many might say I'm entitled to feel that way considering the way she acts, I think I have a bigger issue. I think I'm hurt or something that you aren't the one telling her to back off, that you don't shut her down completely. Why, Erik? That's the bigger issue right now. Why do you let her get away with it? It looks bad when I compare it to your words of love toward me. And I promise, I have never, and will never use the words 'if you loved me, you would ____.' But I must tell you, it's more than my jealousy here. It's also a touch of you not walking away from such a blatant, fake cu—" And before I could get the next two letters out of my mouth, my throat dried up from my long string of words and I coughed and choked until Erik grabbed his water bottle and offered it to me.

"Are you finished talking, or are we taking a break? I need to know if I'm up," he said with a small chuckle.

Damn him for being adorable and lovable and hard to stay upset with. "You're up. I think I've said enough." I tried to say it nonchalantly, but I was anything but nonchalant. I placed my hand over my heart to make sure it wasn't going to pound out of my chest and splatter all over the magnificent wood floors.

It was Erik's turn to take a deep breath. "Sara, no matter what, I do love you. I know it's only been a short time. I know you're frightened. I know you don't trust me totally, and I think I get it, but help me out here. I'm a guy. I'm a guy in recovery who tries to live by the Twelve Steps, especially the Twelfth Step itself. Carry the message. Help others. I know Drea is completely in the wrong here, but she's also someone in trouble. I don't think her drinking is just a ploy to get near me. I believe she really does have a problem and I can't turn my back on that. Not yet. And I *would* have said something this morning in the parking lot, but there were a lot of people around and that was not the time or place for that conversation. Drea took off after the incident without saying a word to me, so I never had a chance to say any of those words you want me to say to her."

My hand was still on my chest, trying to calm my heartbeat. I took my other hand and put it on Erik's chest over his heart. I wasn't surprised that it was pounding almost as hard as mine had been. I looked up into his eyes and gently cupped his face with my hands, pulled his head toward mine, and kissed him. I kissed him deep. I kissed him with love. I kissed him with the knowledge that maybe, just maybe, he did get it. And maybe I could let myself relax a little.

We kissed until my stomach reminded me that it was long past dinner by this point. "I need to get back, and you need to get back to getting ready to go. Text me later when you're in bed so I can say a proper farewell."

His eyes lit up. "A proper farewell? Is that code for sexting? Are we going to sext?"

I kissed his wolf smile goodbye and ran back home feeling better than I had in a while. I think that's what they'd call hope.

CHAPTER 14

The next morning, my eyes opened at the crack of dawn, and I felt a little lighter than I had the day before. Molly was still sound asleep, and there were no sounds coming from the attic room above me. I let my mind wander a little bit, and Erik's handsome face floated into my consciousness. I thought about how we left things and I was feeling cozy and warm and hopeful I might get another hour or two of sleep, but no. It wasn't long before my bladder got me up.

Molly didn't seem to want to rush out of bed, so I took my time in the bathroom, flipping on the shower radio while washing my hair and shaving my legs. I was hoping to hear a weather report for the day and plan accordingly. In the meantime, I softly sang along with Stevie Nicks and soaped up my leg.

As "Landslide" came to a close, and my off-key singing

ended, the DJ started talking about a storm out in the Atlantic that had the potential to hit the Jersey shore harshly.

"Just a heads-up, folks. There's probably fifteen different tracks this storm could take at this point. The weather guys say to wait another twelve hours before a better formed tracking is confirmed. This could be a big one!" The DJ sounded excited at some potentially dangerous news, and I paused in my hair lathering to worry for a moment. Realizing there was nothing I could do at this point, I rinsed my hair and added conditioner before rinsing again and stepping out of the shower. I heard Dani roaming around upstairs and quickly dried off, wrapped a towel around me, and went back to my bedroom in case she wanted to use the bathroom. I heard her come downstairs and call out a good morning through the door. I was surprised to hear how awake she sounded.

"Good morning!" I called back through the door. I heard the bathroom door close and went back to towel drying my hair. It was already humid; I could tell by the waves forming in my hair. I pulled a sundress over my head, a nice, soft black T-shirt material that felt great against my newly shaved legs. The black accentuated my tan. A few flicks of waterproof mascara and I felt like I could meet the heat and haze of the day without flinching.

I twirled around in front of the mirror and gave myself props for looking good in a beachy casual way. *Who're you dressing up for?* asked one of those nagging voices in my head. *Your boyfriend is gone, remember?* it continued. I blew my reflection a kiss and went downstairs to put on a pot of coffee. Dani was nowhere to be seen and Molly was still asleep on my bed upstairs, so Tank and I took our morning walk alone. It looked like it was going to be a lovely, warm day, despite the humidity. Each morning, I noticed more people walking and knew it was only a matter of days before the boards in front of the Pendleton would be filled with humans of all ages. As we passed one of the beach entrances, I couldn't help but overhear three women having a conversation about the storm I'd heard about earlier.

"Bart. They named it, and now it's officially a hurricane." "Is it going to hit here?" "They aren't positive yet, but it could." "Tomorrow night." "Well, crap, my family is supposed to come this weekend." "I hope it doesn't interfere with my party. I heard just flooding and winds."

Their voices faded as I passed them, and my worry kicked in again. That's when I realized if the hurricane did hit us, I'd be dealing with it without Erik. And I was responsible for his daughter and his dog. My coffee started churning around in my belly and I tugged on Tank's leash and turned us around to get back to the Pendleton and check out this Bart asshole for myself.

As we approached the house, I saw Dani and Molly coming out for a walk. "Good morning!" I called. "Did you sleep okay?"

"Yeah, it's really cool up there. Could you hear my TV?"

"Nope, never heard anything. Hey, did you hear anything on TV about this storm that might hit us this week?"

"No, sorry. I was watching Netflix. What kind of storm?" Dani's eyes were as wide as saucers.

Molly picked that moment to whine and pull on the leash, and judging from the very earnest look in Molly's eyes, there was no time to fill Dani in on Bart. "I'll tell you when you get back. I'll get the dogs fed. Feel like breakfast? I know it's a little early."

"Not yet!" Dani called from the end of the front boardwalk, her voice fading as Molly pulled her away.

When Dani got back, we each grabbed a cup of coffee and curled up on the living room chairs. I flipped on the TV and searched for a weather report.

"…models have this storm strengthening over the next couple of days and could hit the Jersey shore as an extra-tropical storm, enough to cause some major flooding and power outages due to the high winds. We're keeping a close eye on this one, folks, and will let you know if any evacuations should take place." The handsome weatherman gifted viewers with a small, concerned smile, but I could see the excitement in his eyes. Weather people really got off on the weather.

Dani looked over at me with her eyes ripped wide open. "Sara, are we concerned about this? Maybe we should tell Dad to come back. Maybe we should go north and get a hotel? What if the power goes out? What if the house floods? We're right here on the beach with nothing but a dune between us and the waves!"

I made a mental note to make sure Dani's future cups of coffee were decaf. "It's not even confirmed that it will hit here. Let's not get too scared yet. We'll watch again later, and tomorrow and when they know more, we'll take whatever action we need to take."

I heard my words coming out of my mouth and they

sounded very grown up. Very responsible. "How about some pancakes?" I asked, forcing my voice not to shake, because truth be told, I was a little nervous myself. Maybe because I was still fragile over Drea and Erik and now this storm. Sometimes the smallest thing could tip you over the edge of grown up and responsible, into a teary mess of anxiety.

Dani's eyes had gone from ripped wide open to relaxed and her mouth curved upwards. "I love pancakes. What kind of syrup do you have? We have real Vermont maple syrup next door if you don't have it!"

Hurricane forgotten, Dani was already walking to the kitchen by the time I answered that I did, in fact, have real maple syrup.

After breakfast and cleaning up the kitchen, I suggested we go grocery shopping and stock up on lots of snacks and goodies for our girls' week. "That way we'll be covered for junk food in case the storm gets bad, and we're stuck inside," I said half-jokingly and started doing an inventory of the refrigerator.

Thirty minutes later we were walking the aisles of the grocery store, throwing not only *needs*, but also *wants* into the cart. The store was definitely more crowded than usual, and we heard rumblings of conversations about the storm. Thirty minutes after that we were back in the Bug and headed to the Pendleton. Molly and Tank met us at the back door, making it difficult to juggle getting my key out of the door lock, open the door, and try not to drop the bags I was holding.

Huffing up the stairs behind me, Dani asked, "Sara, what if

we lose power? All this food could go bad." A worried frown crossed her face.

"We just eat the ice cream and popsicles first. Simple." I gave her a reassuring smile. "Kidding. There's a whole house generator that kicks on automatically if we lose power, remember? But I wouldn't mind eating all the ice cream first just in case."

We worked together putting the groceries away in their proper spots and were done in no time flat. I looked at the kitchen clock and turned to Dani. "Okay, I'm going to dig out the binder for the Pendleton and see if there are instructions for what to do in a storm." No sense waiting until the last minute to learn important crap.

I opened the desk drawer and pulled out the three-ring binder with everything you could ever possibly want to know about the house and the surrounding area: instructions for the TV and remote, garbage pickup, recycling, how to troubleshoot the air conditioning and heat, plus local menus and recommendations for a few local restaurants and every manual for every appliance. And finally, what to do in case of a storm.

I read about the generator and learned how to operate the hurricane shutters. I reviewed the escape routes both from the house and the roads out, which changed depending on how severe the flooding might be.

Confident that I was as ready as I could ever be, I went over what I'd learned with Dani, so that we were both on the same page should something bad happen.

"You know, it could just be a big nothingburger and we end up with a rainy day or two," I said, seeing the worry play out on Dani's face. "And we're as ready as we can be. So let's stop thinking about what might happen and enjoy the day."

It was barely noon, and the sun was warm, the humidity still rising. It would be a perfect beach day since the winds were lightly blowing off the ocean.

Dani's phone chirped with an incoming text, and I watched her grin as she read it. "Tristan wants to take me crabbing on the pier. Is it okay?"

"Absolutely! If you guys catch a few, I'll cook them for us tonight." I watched Dani run upstairs to change into better suited crabbing clothes and trot down the boards to meet Tristan. "Text me later!" I called out to her, and she waved to me in acknowledgment.

That left me to my own devices, and I thought about bringing a towel down to the ocean and meditating for a bit, but I could already see that foot traffic on the boards was increasing, which meant the beach would start filling up. I decided to go for another long walk to think about the words Erik and I had said to each other yesterday. My glimmer of hope from the evening before had dampened a little in the light of day. Erik's arms weren't around me; his lips weren't right there in my ear saying perfect words. The monolith of Drea's house staring me in the face cemented my decision to walk. I decided to change into shorts and a tank top. The wind was blowing gently, but enough to make a sundress fly up unexpectedly. My favorite flip-flops on my feet, I put my house keys in my pocket and set off north on the boards.

One of the beachfront homes along the way was an old Victorian, much like the Pendleton yet not restored to its former glory. The yard, and I say "yard" but it didn't resemble one, because it wasn't exactly the average sandy, beach grass, pilings, and patio furniture type yards you normally see. No, this one was unique and quirky, and one of the larger beachfront properties. Cement statues were scattered around the area in the front of the house, which stood dark and a little bit foreboding. Plants grew wild, seemingly without direction, and filled the spaces between statues and birdbaths with their vines and flowers. Wind chimes of all shapes and sizes and dangling crystals dotted the front porch. It was beautiful chaos, a house I couldn't help but be drawn to, and I loved walking this direction because it gave me the opportunity to see if anything new had been added to the menagerie of statues.

I looked around hoping to see the person or persons who lived there, but there was never anyone around. I wondered when they did all the work associated with the chaotic beauty. My eyes traveled around, enjoying the explosions of color that met my gaze. The boards were absent of walkers down this far, and it was the perfect spot for that meditation I so desperately yearned for. I took a deep breath and closed my eyes, taking in the scent of flowers and the sounds of the wind chimes against the pounding of the ocean waves. Exhaling, I felt some of the stress once again leaving my body, much like it did when Erik held me close. My brain quieted and a sense of peace came over my body.

"Feel better?" a soft voice asked from nearby.

That startled me enough that I choked on my own saliva and coughed, and I looked around to see where the voice came from. From the yard in front of me, a small chuckle erupted. A few feet away stood an older woman with white hair that reached to her waist, straight and full and surrounding her smiling face like sunlight. She was dressed in a flowing caftan of color that reached her ankles, her bare feet peeking from the sand.

"I'm sorry," she continued. "I scared you."

"No, no!" I stammered after getting my voice back. "I was so taken by your property that I had to stop, and the urge to meditate came over me so unexpectedly. It's just so magical."

The woman smiled and repeated her question. "Do you feel better now?"

I paused and took inventory of my innards. I felt calmer. I felt quite zen if I had to pin a feeling on what was going on in my body. "I do," I replied honestly. "Your yard was exactly what I needed. Thank you. I'm Sara." I stuck my hand out to her, which she took in both of hers. A short burst of warmth filled our hands.

"It's nice to meet you, Sara. I'm Lily. I hope you can stay a moment. I don't get too many visitors." Her voice dropped to a whisper. "I think people think I'm weird." Her laugh told me she was kidding, but I didn't doubt her neighbors thought her strange.

"Only if you promise to give me a tour and tell me about all this fabulous stuff," I replied, my hands gesturing around me.

"You must be an artist," Lily said. "I find that only creative people appreciate my home for what it is, instead of calling it an eyesore or even worse, 'interesting.'"

I smiled at her and followed her pointed finger to a gate

leading into her gardens. "I am an artist! And I do very much appreciate this. The work involved must be tremendous to keep this from being horribly overgrown, but I have been walking by here almost daily and—"

"With your golden retriever," she interrupted with another laugh. "Sorry, I love that breed and always look out for them. Go ahead."

"I was only going to say, when do you do all this? I've never seen you in your yard before now."

Lily looked down at the sand and explained that she was a night owl and preferred to garden by moonlight. "It wouldn't be unusual for you to find me out here well after midnight, which explains why you haven't noticed me before this. It's rather unusual that I'm out here right now, as a matter of fact. But something drew me out."

Her face seemed to shift slightly before my eyes. How old is she? I wondered. Over the past few moments in the changing light between the plants and cement, she'd changed from looking like she was in her seventies to appearing to be *maybe* fifties and then back again.

Lily's sharp blue eyes met mine. "Come. Meet my friends."

I wondered for a moment if there was even room for more people in the garden but then realized she was talking about the statues. Lily and I walked around as she said the name of each thing she touched with a caress of her hand. She pressed her forehead against the hard cement, seeming to communicate with each statue.

There was a feeling of magic in this garden. My cares and worries drifted away as we strolled and chatted and as I was introduced to each special thing. Mixed with the smell of the sea and salt air was the scent of burning incense and even though it was the middle of the day, mere footsteps away from the people on the boards and beach, I felt all that flow away. I gazed at Lily, and she gazed back for what seemed like an hour. Something passed between us, an understanding of some sort, a recognition maybe.

"Sara, can I offer you a reading? I feel very strongly that there's a message you need to hear. Something you were meditating about, perhaps?"

I heard myself saying yes and Lily took my hand and led me to a small patio table and chairs tucked away behind a shield of scrub pines. After we sat, she opened a lightly tied silk scarf revealing a well-worn tarot deck. She handed me the deck and told me to shuffle it. As she laid out three cards in front of her, chills started at the top of my head. I've had many a tarot reading at county fairs and none of them ever gave me head chills.

Lily laid out three cards and laid three more on top. As she turned each one over, she explained what the card represented. Laughing, she asked me if I had a new man in my life.

"I do," I responded with a blush.

"And you are in love with this man," she continued.

"I am," I replied, but there was a little catch in my voice and Lily looked up from the card with a questioning look.

"Who are you so jealous of, Sara?"

After I got done swallowing my tongue, I said, "This is impossible."

Lily laughed her soft laugh again and turned over another card and her face grew serious. "There's a child involved. You must protect them."

Instead of swallowing my tongue, this time it stuck to the roof of my mouth. I thought of Dani and how much I loved her, and I knew I'd protect her against anything. "Dani," I croaked out.

Lily tipped her head to the side and tapped her lip. "Funny, I thought it was a female child. My senses must be a bit off."

I shook my head. "It's Dani with an 'I.' She's very important to me."

Lily looked pleased that her senses were right on target and turned over another card. "Things feel off-balance right now, unsure footing because of this jealousy."

I found myself only nodding, not trusting my voice. Tears filled my eyes and spilled over, streaking my cheeks.

"Let's stop for a moment, Sara," Lily said, taking my hands in hers. I was almost getting used to the strange white heat that briefly flashed in our hands. "Let's talk a little about what I've already turned over. Tell me about the jealousy. Tell me about Dani. Tell me about the new relationship."

I don't know if it was because she was kind, or because she was so understanding, or because she was a witch and had put a spell over me, but I opened my mouth and all the words regurgitated out of me. I told her about Erik, and Dani, and then I told her about Drea. As I spoke, I could feel the emotions each one raised in me. When I spoke of Erik and Dani, Lily's eyes filled with love and were as blue as the sky above. Then I told her about Drea and my mouth dropped as I watched her eyes turn from a calm blue to a stormy green. I blinked rapidly in disbelief, and they were back to blue. Though I tried to tell myself it was a passing shadow, that didn't totally explain why her face was still slightly changing and morphing, her age still indiscernible.

"I think that's it," I said, unable to think of anything else to add. I looked down at my hands, still resting in hers. The sun came through the scrub pines and vines and a white heat came off our clasped hands. There was a moment of heat between our fingers and Lily squeezed my hands and picked up the deck again.

Turning over the remaining cards, she smiled. She pointed to the spread before her and took my hands once more, the white glow of heat sparking again. "Sara, I have so much to tell you, but I feel time is short. I want you to listen closely. This woman is no threat to your love. She is not of substance to him and never will be. Let him come to you and welcome him. This union is true and blessed by the divine. Enjoy your love and don't look back."

She released her grip, the heat disappearing as quickly as it came. All at once Lily looked older again, like an energy drain had occurred. Her eyes were closed, and we both sat very still, and all the sounds that had disappeared during the moments of the reading started up in my ears again. The waves, the sounds of people talking and laughing, screaming as the cold waves splashed tender body parts. The wind blowing softly through the wind chimes. The birds chirping, hidden among the plants and vines. I was back from wherever Lily had transported us to.

"Lily?" I asked, wondering if she'd fallen asleep from exhaustion. Her eyes flickered open, and I blew out a sigh of relief that I hadn't accidentally killed her.

Laughing, she stood up from the table. "Go on home, Sara. Never been a reading that killed me yet."

It dawned on me that I hadn't said those words out loud. And as I stood up, I heard her chuckle again.

When I reached the gate, I turned around to ask Lily if I owed her anything for the magic she shared with me, but she was gone. I called out a thank-you, but only the wind chimes answered.

∼

Shortly after I arrived home, I heard the kids walking down the side of the house, laughing and talking and struggling with a basket that looked to be filled with blue claw crabs.

"Sara!" they called in unison. "Look at all the crabs!" and then dissolved in laughter again, delighted with how many they caught.

I met them by the garage and checked out their haul. Certainly too many for the three of us. There were at least fifty good-sized crabs in the basket, all the ones on top scattering around the backs of the others beneath them, trying to escape.

"I guess we'd better think about who to invite to dinner tonight," I said. "Tristan, are your mom and Rachel available?" Other than Drea there was no one else I could think of. I allowed myself a brief but satisfying vision of crabs pinching her on various body parts.

"They're at some dinner function tonight. I was hoping to crash here to eat with you guys," Tristan answered.

That left Drea and that wasn't going to happen. Lily's words left me feeling better about Erik, but I wasn't about to invite the viper into my garden.

"I guess it's just the three of us," I said. "I know you can freeze them after cooking, so help me find a big crab pot and we'll get the water boiling. By the time it boils it'll be dinnertime. Good thing I stocked up on butter." I headed to the kitchen to dig out the food vacuum sealer machine I knew must live here because I found the manual for it while searching for the storm needs.

Two hours later, we were sitting at the dining room table amid a carnage of crab shells. I don't remember the last time I felt that full, and judging by the two faces opposite me, Dani and Tristan felt the same way. Mild groans escaped their buttery lips, and I laughed at them. They, in turn, pointed at my face and laughed back. I'm guessing I was just as buttery.

Later that evening, after Tristan went home, after cleaning crabs, cleaning the kitchen, and cleaning ourselves, Dani and I walked the dogs. We didn't walk far enough to see Lily's house, but I told Dani all about my visit with her.

Entranced with the story, Dani latched onto the advice Lily had given me. "So now you have to feel better, Sara!" she exclaimed. "I mean, a complete stranger who just happens to be psychic, who just happens to be out in her garden when you're standing there, that's pretty amazing!"

"It felt amazing to hear it, I must say. She was quite magical, and the entire experience was a little bit surreal."

"Did you tell my dad yet?" Dani asked.

"Not yet. I got a text from him earlier that he was doing back-to-back signings in DC and he'd be in touch later when things quieted down."

"You're going to tell him what she said, right?"

"Absolutely. Don't worry. I'm feeling much better about everything than I was before."

Once the words were out of my mouth, I realized how much better I did feel. Drea no longer seemed to be at the threat level I'd previously assigned her. My footing with Erik felt strong. I didn't even bother wondering where this mindset came from. I knew exactly why I felt better. My mind was open to magic, all kinds of magic.

CHAPTER 15

I was lying in bed having an email conversation with the Cell about all the happenings in our lives when my phone dinged with an incoming text.

ERIK
Sara, are you there?

SARA
I am.

ERIK
I miss you so much already and it's only been one day.

SARA
Same. I have so much to tell you and I wish I could do it in person.

> **ERIK**
> I hope it's good. Things are going a little rocky here with venues canceling because of some storm coming in. I could use some good news.

> **SARA**
> Oh, it's good.

> **ERIK**
> Phew. So, tell me.

I chewed on my lip for a moment trying to decide what my words would be.

> **SARA**
> I love you. I believe you. I believe *in* you. And I'm sorry.

> **ERIK**
> Baby, I love you too. Don't apologize for your feelings, but I'm glad we're on the same page again.

After a few more minutes of gooey texting, we said our good nights. I let out a sigh of contentment and stroked Molly's soft fur. I closed my eyes and imagined Erik coming home. Home to me. Home to Dani. Being back in his arms again.

That's when my phone decided to erupt with an ear-splitting alert, practically levitating me off the bed. It was the emergency alert system letting me know that good old Bart was going to have some impact on our little patch of paradise. From the floor above me I heard the same alert sound on

Dani's phone, and then the sound of her footsteps pounding down the stairs and across the hall to my bedroom.

"Sara? You awake?" Dani knocked softly on my door.

"You didn't think I could sleep through that alert, did you? Come in."

Dani got into bed beside me, and we read the weather statement together. Bart was now quickly taking a path that would soon cause us some high winds and flooding. Apparently, the biggest problem was that a new moon at the time of impact to our area would cause increased flooding concerns. Power outages expected from the winds. We were still a day or so away from major issues, but ocean levels were already up, and I could hear the wind whipping occasionally outside my window. The thought popped into my head that it must be very noisy at Lily's house with all the wind chimes ringing at once.

Dani looked at me with saucer eyes. "Sara, should we evacuate?"

"We haven't gotten any evacuation orders and I know they would already be knocking at our door if we had to get out. We have that huge dune protecting us, and we sit very far back from the boardwalk, so it would take a really big storm surge to hit us here at the house."

I hoped my words calmed her a bit because one of us needed to be calm right now. And I really wished Erik were home.

"Let's go downstairs and watch the weather on TV. I don't know about you but after hearing that alert I doubt I'm going back to sleep anytime soon. I'll make some tea."

Dani agreed and downstairs we went as the wind whistled.

It was after midnight when Dani and I were sufficiently comforted by the weather report. They expected some generalized road flooding, but evacuation was left up to the person. Over the years, the Pendleton had withstood many storms and seemed no worse for wear. I sent Dani up the stairs to her bedroom and sent a quick text to Rachel to see if she was still awake.

SARA

> Hey Rachel, it's Sara. Are you still awake by any chance?

RACHEL

> Who could sleep in this wind?

SARA

> Right? In case the power goes out, please grab Lisa, Tristan, and Tosh and come here. We have a whole house generator and tons of bedrooms. If it doesn't flood to the house.

RACHEL

> Okay, thank you, we may take you up on that.

I pondered my next move. Do I invite the vixen into my home or let her ride out the storm with her built-in floaty devices? My empathy bone wouldn't let me leave her be. I let out a sigh and resigned myself to the text, until I realized I didn't have Drea's phone number. Erik did though, and I took another chance at finding my guy awake.

> SARA
> Hey, you awake?

> ERIK
> Who could sleep in this wind?

After making sure I wasn't reading Rachel's text, I laughed.

> SARA
> The storm is getting worse quickly and I invited Rachel, Tristan, and Lisa to come over if power goes out. And I guess I have to offer the same thing to Drea damn it.

> ERIK
> That's a big step, baby!

> SARA
> Yeah. We'll see. But I don't have her number. Can you text it to me?

> ERIK
> Sure. Listen the rest of the tour was postponed because of Bart, and I'll be home as soon as I can get there. I love you.

> SARA
> Yay! Be careful. I love you. Keep in touch.

I chewed my lip again. Drea and I didn't exactly leave things in a healthy state at our last meeting. I could text Rachel back and tell her to swing in and bring Drea along with them. Or I could be the bigger person and just invite her. I let go of my lower lip, took a deep breath in, and whooshed it out again.

SARA
Hi Drea, it's Sara next door. I have a generator in case power goes out and you are welcome to join us if that happens.

DREA
Is Erik home?

Seriously this woman was going to make me regret sending that text.

SARA
Not yet, why?

DREA
Just wondering. I'll keep your offer in mind.

Not even a thanks. I should have left her to her floaties.

I knew sleep was going to be elusive. The ocean was crashing against the shore and the wind was whipping in from the southeast just as the weatherman predicted. I went upstairs to my bedroom where Molly was sound asleep in bed. When I grabbed my pillow and the quilt, she raised her head slightly and gave me a look because I interrupted her slumber. I turned off my bedroom light hoping to see the waves, but nothing was visible past my front walk. The windows of the house were rattling and for a brief moment I regretted not at least thinking about evacuating. Remembering the hurricane shutters, I ran downstairs with my bedding, threw everything on the couch, and activated all the windows on the east to shut.

I was just patting myself on the back for doing that when a scream came from the third floor and I heard Dani running down the stairs.

"What was that?" she cried. "Something was happening outside my window!"

"Crap. I'm sorry. It was the hurricane shutters activating against the wind. I should have let you know. Never realized they would be that loud."

Dani let out a held breath and laughed. She saw my pillow and quilt on the couch and asked if she could join me.

"Absolutely. Go upstairs and get your pillow and blanket. You can have the recliner. I have to warn you that I invited our neighbors to come stay here if the power goes out."

Dani's eyes narrowed. "Neighbors like Tristan? Or neighbors like Drea?"

"All of the above. This isn't the time to turn our backs on someone. And for some reason I was feeling sorry for her, so I just did it."

"Oooookay," she replied. "This could get interesting."

"Oh, and I forgot to tell you, your dad is on his way home. The rest of the book tour got postponed because of this crap." I gestured my arms around me at the wind, rain, and pounding surf.

"Oh good!" she exclaimed. "That makes me feel better." Then her face darkened a bit when she realized he would have to navigate this storm to reach us. "He'll be okay, right?"

"I have no doubt he'll reach us without issue. If the roads are flooded, he can park and walk in through the properties." I sounded more confident than I felt, but why worry Dani? I was almost hoping the power would go out so we'd have more people around us helping to make decisions and creating a buffer between me and Drea.

And that's when the universe laughed at me and the world around me went dark. Very, very dark.

"Hold still, the generator takes about ten seconds to kick on."

Sure enough, by the time I got the words out and turned my cell phone's flashlight on, the lights flickered on, and the hum of the house was heard once again. Cable was out; the TV was black and showing a "No connection" error message. I looked at my cell phone screen and saw that Wi-Fi was out.

"Okay, go get your stuff and we'll camp out here and see if we get company."

Dani ran upstairs and Tank shuffled into the living room from the kitchen. He and Molly seemed completely unfazed by the storm. He yawned and found a spot near my feet to curl up. No sooner did he get comfortable, when a pounding on the back door brought us both to attention and Tank running to the kitchen as fast as his stumpy legs could carry him, barking all the way.

I assumed it was Drea or Lisa and wondered why they didn't approach the house from the boardwalk. I flipped on the back door porch light and could make out a solitary figure, a hood up against the wind and rain. Not Drea. I held Tank back by his collar and opened the door. The hooded figure turned toward me, and I muffled a gasp as Ron waved and gave me a sickly smile. I quickly composed my face because I had no doubt it wasn't a happy one.

Once inside, he took off his raincoat and I handed him a dish towel to dry his face and hands. Figuring it would be a long night, I started a pot of coffee.

"Thanks." Ron handed me the damp towel back and I tossed it down to the laundry. "I'm really sorry to barge in here like this, Sara. Honestly this is the last place I want to be." He took a breath. "I tried making it home from Atlantic City, but this was as far as I could get. In fact, my car is two blocks away in a parking lot."

"Where's Bronwyn? Did you leave her in the car?"

Ron lowered his head. "She's not with me. She kicked me out." His face crumpled a bit and for a moment I was a-scared he was going to cry. "I did something stupid, and she found out and I left without my suitcase, and I tried to get home…" His voice trailed off as his story had reached full circle, minus some of the juicy details. "So I had no choice, Sara. Nothing is open and power is out all over."

"Relax. I'm not going to throw you out. Let me see if I have a pair of large sweatpants and socks for you. Yours are leaving puddles on my kitchen floor."

"Oh God, thank you, Sara." The relief in his voice was palpable. Molly must have heard his voice from upstairs, and she came running into the kitchen, sliding on the wet floor, and plowed straight into Ron.

I stifled a laugh and went upstairs to look for clothes. On my way up, I passed Dani on her way down, pillow and blanket in her arms.

"Did I hear pounding on the back door?" she asked. "Was it Tristan?"

"Sorry to disappoint you. It's even more exciting. My ex-husband Ron," I said sarcastically.

Dani laughed and I told her I'd fill her in later and went through my stretchy pants and socks for Ron. The socks were no problem, I had a pair of the one-size-fits-all, bright green slipper socks with treads, which would be stretchy enough to fit him. The pants were another story. I found one pair of sweatpants that might possibly do. They were for those days when I felt like a busted can of biscuits. I chuckled because they were purple with aqua flowers all over them and would certainly enhance Ron's squinty, lying eyes. Before going back downstairs, I texted Erik that the power was out, and my ex-husband was in. I didn't get an immediate response and was relieved, hoping he was driving home.

I threw the clothing at Ron and pointed to the bathroom. "You can change in there. When you're done, you can go downstairs and put your wet things in the dryer."

When Ron emerged from the bathroom, he did as instructed then joined us in the living room.

Dani was able to contain her laughter, but I wasn't. His shirt, hidden previously by his raincoat, was a pink Izod golf shirt. It went amazingly well with the purple and aqua sweatpants and lime green slipper socks. I slowly lifted my cell phone and snuck a picture.

"SARA, NO!" Ron shouted when he realized what I'd done.

"Sorry. It's just too perfect." One touch of a button and

that photo was on its way to the Cell. They needed to see this too.

At 2:00 a.m. we were all still awake, reading and trying to get the most current reports on our phones. So far, the cell towers were still up and running. The hurricane shutters were holding against the winds, which never seemed to let up. The surf sounded like it was at our doorway, but I couldn't see far enough into the night to find out how close the sea was to our front door. The shutters blocked our view of the ocean, and I couldn't tell if the dune had been breached. In the distance I heard sirens and a shiver went through me as I thought about Erik making his way back from DC in the storm.

More pounding on the back door brought all three of us to our feet and heading to the kitchen. Tristan waved at me through the glass, and I opened the door and let the three of them in, plus a very drenched Tosh. Dani grabbed towels from the linen closet and handed them out to Lisa, Rachel, and Tristan. She kept one and used it to try to dry Tosh, but she was more interested in shaking water all over the kitchen and sniffing at Molly and Tank.

"I've never seen anything like this in my life!" Lisa cried. "This is amazing and scary at the same time."

"The streets are flooding. The ocean breached where the dune ends at the beach entrance. We had to wade through almost a foot of water until we got to the interior of the block."

That was the moment the three of them caught sight of Ron, who was hovering in the background. I watched them try to mask their reaction to his outfit then patted myself on the back again and thanked the universe for providing me this entertaining distraction from the storm. After I introduced everyone, we headed to the living room. I made more coffee and pulled some snacks out of the cabinets to offer our guests.

"I told Drea to come also, but I haven't heard from her. You didn't see any activity at her house, did you?"

All three shook their heads no. "Maybe I should text her again," I said. Before I could blink, lightning lit up the sky and through one window we could see a figure on the side of our house, struggling against the wind and rain. "Why do I feel like that's her out there?" I shook my head.

"Someone should go help her," Rachel said. Everyone murmured in agreement, but nobody moved.

"We can't leave her out there, that's insane!" Ron exclaimed, and he struggled to get into his raincoat and looked around for his shoes.

I pointed in their general direction. "Go for it. She's just your type." There may have been a little bit of pettiness in my voice. "Keep in mind those are the only dry pants I have that will fit you. If you get them wet, you'll be sitting in your underwear, or my pink fluffy robe."

Ron looked down and pulled the sweatpants up over his knees. He pushed his stocking clad feet into his ruined leather loafers. "Someone has to help her," he repeated. The rest of us just nodded and I pointed to the back door. He shook his head, grabbed a flashlight, and opened the door, almost losing it in the wind. As he disappeared into the dark, we all crowded around the window to see if Drea, if that actually was Drea, would make it safely to the Pendleton.

We could see the faint glimmer of the flashlight against the rain, and the occasional lightning strike would give us a brief glimpse of the storm. The flashlight reached the struggling figure, and the light started moving back toward us. It felt like forever, but finally the two figures burst through the back door.

Ron, his ruined loafers squishing water and the rain coming off his coat, left more puddles on the floor, and the dogs were having a blast sliding and running around. The figure behind Ron moved forward, and indeed, it was Drea. She was shivering in her light jacket, and her high heels matched her gauzy nightgown underneath. Her normally perfect beach hair was dripping wet, and her eyelashes appeared to be stuck sideways on her eyes. Even Tank took a double take before barking at her.

"Are you okay?" Ron asked, handing Drea one of the few dry towels left. "Here, let me help." He grabbed one end of the towel and was patting her down like a professional. As she slipped out of her jacket, Ron's hands started to shake a little as the double Ds came prominently into view.

"Oh, sweetie!" Drea purred. "You saved me. I don't think I could have made it without you." She gave him one of her glittery smiles and touched his arm.

I watched as she turned on her charm, usually reserved for Erik. Had the viper found a new victim? Was she ready to admit that Erik was out of her reach?

"Drea, this is Ron, my ex-husband. Ron, this is Drea, my next-door neighbor." Ron looked Drea up and down like he was evaluating a sample cut of deli meat at the supermarket.

"Drea, a pleasure." Taking her hand, he kissed the back of it. "Let me help you with these," he said as he pulled her eyelashes off her temples. "You were walking straight into the wind for a bit, weren't you?"

Drea paused, evaluating the prospect in front of her. Obviously, the outfit was a deterrent and had I known this prior, I may have not given him my most ridiculous outfit to wear. Her eyes focused on his face, and she seemed pleasantly surprised to find him similarly focused on hers.

I watched something spark between them and could barely hold back my laughter. The two of them deserved each other more than I could have ever hoped. I thanked the universe again as the thunder rolled and the winds seemed to shake the entire house.

We spent the next few hours in various states of sleeping, reading, eating, and talking. I pulled out some board games and the hours passed by as the storm started to lessen.

At dawn I wrapped my coat around me and slipped into rain boots. The dogs were anxious to go out after a long night avoiding the prospect of being out in the storm. I leashed Molly and Tank and found Tosh's lead to hook on her collar. We struggled our way out the back door into the driveway, which was rutted and washed out in several places. Beach grass, uprooted from the dunes, dotted the ground everywhere. The winds were much lighter, and the sky was a brighter gray than I expected. With the exception of the driveway washout and the beach grass, this part of the house seemed to have come through Bart just fine.

The dogs reminded me that we were on a mission and I turned to untangle leashes, catching my boot in one of those new ruts. As I fell, wrapped in leashes, I saw Erik at the end of the driveway. I managed to wave as I went down, hoping it didn't look as bad as it was. I let go of the leashes before I broke a bone, and all three dogs ran to Erik. Of course, Molly got there first so the rest was kind of like doggy déjà vu.

As I lay in the driveway, struggling to get my boot out of the rut, I watched Erik try to stand after being licked and jumped on by the three beasts. He grabbed the leashes and started toward me, his hand reaching down to help me up.

"You're here," I said, tears filling my eyes. "You're safe."

"I am. It was a wild ride getting here and a long walk from the unflooded area, but I'm here."

Holding my hands, he pulled me to him, kissing me and murmuring wonderful words that made me ache for him.

I heard the back door open, and Dani ran out to see her dad. She flew into his arms and hugged him as hard as she could. He handed her the leashes and asked her to hold the dogs for a moment.

Erik took my hands again and kneeled in front of me, his knees deep in water-filled ruts. Slipping his hand into his coat pocket, he pulled out a small black velvet box.

I'm pretty sure I was breathing, but time seemed to move in slow motion as he opened the box and I saw the sparkling square-cut vintage diamond ring it held.

"Sara. I'm not waiting any longer. I've been wanting to do this since the moment I met you. I love you. Will you marry me?"

Time, which had been moving so slowly, stopped completely as the man of my dreams asked me for my hand in marriage.

Dani squealed as I whispered my yes, and Erik slipped the ring on my finger and kissed it.

"Our love is true, Sara. I promise I will make you the happiest woman on earth. I promise to make you laugh every day and support you in everything you do."

I thought how perfectly he said the same words Lily had said.

"And I promise to love you and make you the happiest man on earth."

Dani was done waiting by that point and jumped on both of us, the dogs following behind. She was laughing and crying at the same time, and life seemed pretty dang perfect right at that moment.

"So, who is inside?" Erik asked.

"Rachel, Lisa, Tristan, Drea, and Ron," I answered. "And boy do I have some news for you!" I laughed and Dani poked her dad and agreed as we explained the chemistry between Drea and Ron.

"My God, they're perfectly suited, aren't they?" Erik mused. "I wish them the best."

We went inside and Erik greeted everyone, got introduced to Ron, and to Erik's credit, he never said a word about Ron's outfit.

I raised the hurricane shutters and was pleased that the damage was minimal, mostly displaced sand that would only require a strong back and arms.

Returning outside, Erik and I walked as far as we could before the boardwalk became impassable and we stopped and watched the still churning sea, dark and foamy.

He kissed me under the gray skies, and my world burst into color. I nestled into his arms, and I was home.

ACKNOWLEDGMENTS

Summer of Sara would never have come to fruition without the help of many people. I've saved this for last because I have a terrible fear of who I may leave out.

In the beginning it was all for my Dawgs. My circle of internet friends born on scrapbook messaging boards. Their patient support over the last dozen years has been priceless when all I wanted to do was write them a funny story.

From that circle comes my real-life Cell, Lisa Wallace and Barbara Given. Again, endless cheerleaders. An additional special thanks to Barb for creating the exquisite art used on the cover. The moment I saw it I knew it would be perfect.

My bonus daughter Heidi. *Summer of Sara* was stalled at one third through when Heidi asked to read it. I heard her burst out laughing and I knew at that moment it might be good enough to finish. I love you.

Nikki Busch, editor extraordinaire. Years of support, answering all my questions, advice, and an incredible edit. Thank you for helping make this a reality.

My friend Diane Case, for proof reading, I knew I would get a thorough job and you didn't disappoint.

Jonathan Carr of Weather NJ for his help with describing

the storm impacting the Shore and what the weather leading up to Hurricane Bart would look like.

My friend Amy Price, for reading all the versions and offering support, suggestions, and advice. And keeping me grounded during quarantine.

To Rod Picott and Brian Kathenes, thank you for your help, suggestions, phone calls, visits and love. I put all of it to good use.

Leah Marie Kirk for being my partner in crime and for the beautiful author photo.

Jeffrey Metzger for photographing the cover art and being such a perfectionist. And for being such a great friend.

And finally, Jeff. For having the patience to support me through this 100 percent. I love you.

ABOUT THE AUTHOR

Summer of Sara is author Alexandra Rusch's debut novel. "Sandi" lives in gorgeous Warren County NJ with her husband Jeff, and various fur-faces. She is an artist, potter, and a Jersey Girl, born and bred.

If you enjoyed *Summer of Sara*, please consider leaving a review on Amazon, Goodreads, or your favorite review site. Thank you!

Made in the USA
Middletown, DE
07 April 2023